LOCATION AND LAND USE

Publications of the Joint Center for Urban Studies of the Massachusetts Institute of Technology and Harvard University

The Joint Center for Urban Studies, a cooperative venture of the Massachusetts Institute of Technology and Harvard University, was founded in 1959 to do research on urban and regional problems. Participants have included scholars from the fields of architecture, business, engineering, city planning, economics, history, law, philosophy, political science, and sociology. This book is one of a series in which the Joint Center presents its principal findings.

William Alonso

Location and Land Use

TOWARD A GENERAL THEORY OF LAND RENT

HARVARD UNIVERSITY PRESS
Cambridge, Massachusetts
1964

Distributed in Great Britain by Oxford University Press, London

Library of Congress Catalog Card Number 63-17193

Printed in the United States of America

Distributed by Harvard University Press, Cambridge 38, Massachusetts

Preface

This work developed out of a sense that there might be value in generalizing and articulating with care the classic theory of rent and location that has been in the air for a century and a half. At first I thought that a codifying of certain basic relations and simple statistical tests would suffice, but these simple relations proved to have some wrinkles that would not iron out. I was then led back to their assumptions, and to reassembling these into a consistent whole. This was a lengthy process, and the deductive chain would often become tangled; but untangling the knots has been a most enjoyable and instructive labor.

The method is that of economics, and the concern ultimately geographic. I have used the notation of mathematics because it makes possible clear and concise statements of logical connections, but I have paralleled the mathematical analysis as far as possible with a presentation in words and diagrams, both for the benefit of readers interested in the subject but lacking the mathematics, and to check to my own satisfaction that mathematical sense agreed with common sense. The analysis has led me to conclusions that differ from commonly held opinion concerning urban structure, and it may be that these differences will prove important for city and regional planning. In the meantime, I have been pleased that the earlier presentation of this theory in my doctoral dissertation has been used by several researchers in urban matters.

A word of explanation is necessary about bibliographic references. The first version of this work was completed in 1959, and since that time there has been a torrent of literature related to my subject matter. I have included some new references where they cast new light, but have not attempted systematic coverage. Nothing I have seen disproves the theory presented here, and much supports it.

Acknowledgments

The bulk of this work was developed as a doctoral dissertation in the Department of Regional Science at the University of Pennsylvania, under the stimulating guidance of Walter Isard, and was made possible by a Regional Science Fellowship financed by Resources for the Future. Benjamin H. Stevens deserves my warmest thanks for giving endlessly of his time and helping me in countless ways, from teaching me some mathematics to moral support. For their forbearance in allowing themselves to be subjected to portions of this work, I thank Michael Teitz, Robert Coughlin, Irwin Friend, Eugene Smolensky, and the late Robert Scott-Brown. Thomas Melone and Willard Hansen have my thanks for sending Philadelphia materials halfway around the world to me in Indonesia.

The work was rewritten and reorganized at the Joint Center for Urban Studies of the Massachusetts Institute of Technology and Harvard University and several new sections were developed. I thank Martin Meyerson, who was Director of the Joint Center at that time, and Lloyd Rodwin, Chairman of the Faculty Committee, for their interest and their kind assistance.

Contents

List of Figures

TABLES

LOCATION AND LAND USE

The Economics of Urban Land: Introduction and Review

A. INTRODUCTION

As cities have grown in importance, the various social sciences have become increasingly concerned with them. The internal structure of cities has proved to be a subject of extraordinary richness and of such complexity that only a modest beginning has been made toward its understanding. Why does one have trouble finding a gas station in a downtown area? Why is there a Greenwich Village? Who lives in slums and why? What are the mechanics by which an area which used to be predominantly Italian rapidly becomes Puerto Rican? Why does one not find pawnbrokers in exurbia? How does a mansion become a rooming house? Why is schizophrenia the dominant mental illness in some parts of the city and not in others? A torrent of literature is devoted to these and similar topics, some of it dull, some of it brilliant. Sociologists, economists, geographers, social psychologists, among others, have given currency to expressions such as "succession," "highest and best use," "social symbolism," "hobohemia," "service functions," "ecological processes," "gravity models." The variety of approaches to be found almost matches that of the subject matter.

The approach that will be followed in this study will be that of economics, and from this wealth of subject matter only a pallid skeleton will emerge. Both the Puerto Rican and the Madison Avenue advertising man will be reduced to that uninteresting individual, economic man. The squalor of the pawnbroker and the flair of the exclusive fashion-house will disappear into that grey entity, the firm. The exquisite legal complexities of real estate will vanish into straightforward buying or renting, and the rich topography of the city will flatten to a featureless plain. It is hoped that by this method a self-consistent explanatory theory will be developed which will shed light on some aspects of the internal structure of cities, however incomplete this explanation may be from the point of view of those things which are not considered.

The theory to be presented here concerns the relation of land values to land uses within the city. The focus of attention will be on residential land, which covers four-fifths of all privately developed land in major American cities.[1] There are two reasons for this emphasis. The first, of course, is that residences are the predominant use of land. The second is that the theorists of urban land values and land uses have neglected residential land, and the economic theory of residential land uses must catch up with that of other land uses. On the other hand, urban firms will be examined more briefly. There is a great variety of types of urban firms, affected by diverse factors in their location. The treatment of the firm in these pages will be general, and may be adapted to one type of firm or another. Finally, the theory will be formulated in such a way that it is congruent with the existing theory of agricultural land uses. Urban and agricultural theory will form a unified theory of land uses and land values.

B. Theory of Land Values: Before 1900

The concern of the economists with rent dates at least to the Physiocrats of the 18th century. By rent they meant, as most economists still do, that for agricultural land. It is understandable that their interest should focus on agricultural land and that they should ignore the problems of urban sites. Theirs was an agricultural society, while cities were relatively unimportant in the landscape and viewed as parasitic on the honest toil of agriculture. This unconcern for urban land continued until late in the 19th century, and even now the subject is still a neglected one in spite of the enormous importance that cities have attained. The formal analysis of the problems of urban land is more difficult than that for agriculture. Moreover, the successes of agricultural theory (which will be referred to below and in chapter 3) seem to have fostered preconceptions among the theorists of urban land which often lead

1. Harland Bartholomew, *Land Uses in American Cities* (Cambridge, Mass.: Harvard University Press, 1955), p. 46.

them to pursue unproductive lines of reasoning. Thirdly, land rent as a subject appears to have lost much of its urgency because of increased agricultural productivity and the relative decrease in importance of the agricultural sector in the economies of the more advanced countries (which are the ones which produce economic theory). Finally, the theory in this subject has become bogged down in a Sargasso Sea of conflicting definitions and emphases, and the "anarchic conditions prevailing in this field of study"[2] have greatly hampered the productivity of ideas and the value of discussion.

At the beginning of the 19th century David Ricardo presented a treatment of agricultural rent which is still the foundation of most present-day theory.[3] Ricardo pointed out that the most fertile lands are the first put to use, and that less favored land is put to use as the demand for agricultural products increases. The rent on the most productive land is based on its advantage over the least productive, the competition among farmers insuring that the full advantage go to the landlords in the form of rent. This advantage is equal to the value of the difference in the productivity of land. Ricardo recognized as well that land which is nearer the market bears lower transport costs on its produce than more distant land, and that this advantage also accrues to the landlords in the form of rent as a result of competition among the farmers. However, Ricardo devoted his attention primarily to fertility differentials. A few years later J. H. von Thünen developed the theory of location differential rent more fully.[4] The various agricultural land uses around a market place bid for the use of land, and land is assigned to the highest bidder in each case. The rent each crop can bid at each location will be the savings in transportation of its product that that site affords in contrast with a more distant site. The most distant land in cultivation yields no savings in transportation, and con-

---

2. Carl R. Bye, *Developments and Issues in the Theory of Rent* (New York: Columbia University Press, 1940), p. 104. For a very thorough review of many aspects of the literature on urban land rent, see Max R. Bloom, *Economic Criteria and the Use of Land in Subsidized Urban Redevelopment Areas*, Ph.D. dissertation, The American University, Washington, D.C., 1959.

3. David Ricardo, *On the Principles of Political Economy and Taxation*, 1817. Though his is the most important early treatment, Adam Smith in his *Wealth of Nations*, 1776, already recognized that rent varied with the fertility and situation of land.

4. Johann H. von Thünen, *Der isolierte Staat in Beziehung auf Landwirtschaft und Nationalekonomie* (1st vol., Hamburg, 1826; 3rd vol., and new ed., Hamburg, 1863).

sequently there will be no rent at that location. Viewed another way, the rent at any location is equal to the value of its product minus production costs and transport costs. This approach has recently been fully and formally developed by Dunn and Isard,[5] and will be presented in greater detail in chapter 3.

The early economists had little to say on urban land. Adam Smith says nothing about its valuation, remarking that this land is unproductive and the landlord a monopolist.[6] Neither does Ricardo offer any method for judging its value. J. S. Mill views it as a simple monopoly problem, where the value of a fixed and limited supply of "houses and building ground, in a town of definite extent" will be such that the demand is just sufficient to carry off the supply offered.[7] Alfred Marshall devotes a chapter to urban land values, but concerns himself almost entirely with profit-making land uses, such as retail stores and manufacturing plants. He emphasizes the importance of location within the city, and defines "situation value" as the sum of the money values of the situation advantages of a site. According to Marshall, "site value," the price which a site would fetch if cleared of buildings and sold in the free market, is equal to situation value plus agricultural rent. The various land uses bid for the land, that use capturing the site "from which the most profitable results are anticipated." Marshall considers as well the size of the site in relation to the height of the building upon it, stating that "if land is cheap he [the entrepreneur] will take much of it; if it is dear he will take less and build high." He concludes that "the industrial demand for land is in all respects parallel to the agricultural." That is to say, in the urban as in the agricultural case, potential users of land make bids for various sites based on their respective location advantages, and the highest bidder captures the land in each case.[8] The parallel does not extend to the fertility of land.

5. Edgar S. Dunn, Jr., *The Location of Agricultural Production* (Gainesville: University of Florida Press, 1954); Walter Isard, *Location and Space-Economy* (New York: John Wiley & Sons, 1956).

6. Adam Smith, *The Wealth of Nations* (New York: Dutton, Everyman's Library Edition), vol. I, p. 320, vol. II, p. 325.

7. John Stuart Mill, *Principles of Political Economy* (New York: Longmans, Green), pp. 444, 445, 448, 649.

8. Alfred Marshall, *Principles of Economics* (London: Macmillan, 7th ed., 1916 [1st ed., 1890]). In particular, book V, chap. XI, "Marginal Costs in Relation to Urban Values," and appendix G. The quotations are taken from pp. 445, 448, 450.

Marshall's analysis contains the essentials of present day theory, as we shall see. However, he does not extend his theory to the value of land for residences, and in this respect later theory, too, has been deficient. Moreover, it would seem that later theorists have not studied Marshall's analysis with care, for the question of the size of the site is almost universally ignored. Yet the market equilibrium (in which the market is cleared) must concern itself with quantities as well as with prices. Later writers, however, seem content with considering a location as a dimensionless point, and speak of bidding for a site, paying no attention to its size. The matter can be made very clear at the level of the firm. If two firms realize the same location advantages with respect to a location, but one requires a site only half the size of that required by the other, the former will be able to bid a price per square foot of land at that location twice as large as the latter. Thus, for the purposes of a theory in which the land market is cleared, and for the purposes of determining the bids *per unit of land*, the size of the site must be considered, and the point of location must be given the attribute of extension.[9]

C. Theory of Urban Land Values: After 1900

R. M. Hurd

At the beginning of the present century, activity in this field of theory passed to America. R. M. Hurd published his *Principles of City Land Values* in 1903. In his Preface he states that he found "in economic books merely brief references to city land," and proceeds to outline a theory for urban land which closely resembles that of von Thünen for agriculture:

As a city grows, more remote and hence inferior land must be utilized and the difference in desirability between the two grades produces economic rent in locations of the first grade, but not in those of the second. As land of a still more remote and inferior grade comes into use, ground rent is forced still higher in land of the first grade, rises in land of the second grade, but not in land of the third grade, and so on. Any utility may compete for any location within a city and all land goes to the highest bidder . . . Practically

9. For a discussion on a related topic, see Dunn, *The Location of Agricultural Production*, "Industrial vs. Agricultural Location Theory," pp. 86–92. Dunn points out that agricultural location analysis is carried out at the level of the industry as a whole (for example, the wheat-growing industry), while industrial location analysis is carried out at the level of the firm.

all land within a city earns some economic rent, though it may be small, the final contrast being with the city's rentless and hence, strictly speaking, valueless circumference.

He summarizes:

Since value depends on economic rent, and rent on location, and location on convenience, and convenience on nearness, we may eliminate the intermediate steps and say that value depends on nearness.

Hurd does not, however, consider the size of the site, and bypasses the problem of residential land saying that "the basis of residence values is social and not economic—even though the land goes to the highest bidder." He allows that "where residences contain more than one tenant . . . the basis of value is economic and conforms closely to the principles governing business property," but does not explore the nature of this type of demand or make clear why residences with more than one tenant should differ conceptually from single-family residences.[10]

The Land Economists

Since the 1920's, in connection with the development of city planning, there has arisen in this country a voluminous literature in the field of "land economics." Its principal tenets with respect to urban land values were developed in 1926 by Robert M. Haig. The mechanics of Haig's theory do not seem to differ significantly from Marshall's or Hurd's: "Rent appears as the charge which the owner of a relatively accessible site can impose because of the saving in transport costs which the use of his site makes possible," and a prospective occupant gains the use of a site by outbidding competing users. However, an innovation in the theory is its strong statement of the complementarity of rent and transport costs. Transportation is a device to overcome the "friction of space," and the better the transportation, the less the friction. But, "while trans-

10. Richard M. Hurd, *Principles of City Land Values* (New York: The Record and Guide, 1903). The quotations are taken from pp. 11–12, 13, 77, 78. However, it should be noted that, strictly, the margin of the city will only be valueless if agriculture is excluded from consideration. Von Thünen himself anticipates the extension of his agricultural theory to the urban case: "If we investigate the reasons why site rent increases toward the center of the city, we will find it is the labor saving, the greater convenience and the reduction of the loss of time in connection with the pursuit of business," *Der isolierte Staat*, pp. 212–213, cited in R. T. Ely and G. S. Wehrwein, *Land Economics* (New York: Macmillan, 1940), pp. 444–445.

portation overcomes friction, site rentals and transport costs represent the cost of what friction remains." Thus, the user of a site pays as the "costs of friction" transport costs and rent, which is "the saving in transport costs." But the complementarity of rent and transport costs is limited: "The sum of the two items, the costs of friction, is not constant, however. On the contrary, it varies with the site. The theoretically perfect site for the activity is that which furnishes the desired degree of accessibility at the lowest costs of friction." An interesting hypothesis results from this view: "... the layout of the metropolis ... tends to be determined by a principle which may be termed the minimizing of the costs of friction."[11] Or, in the restatement of a later writer: "... the perfect land market would produce a pattern of land uses in a community which would result in the minimum aggregate land value for the entire community. The most convenient arrangement results in the lowest aggregate transportation costs; in terms of saving of transportation costs, the advantages of the more convenient sites are reduced."[12]

The similarity of this view to Marshall's and Hurd's is clear, but there are dissimilarities as well, arising from Haig's attempt at greater precision. The view of the firm as locating so as to minimize its costs of friction is acceptable in the cases of agriculture and of a manufacturing firm in a market of perfect competition, but it is not acceptable for the case of a retail firm. The volume of sales of a retail store will vary with its location, and the firm must weigh the costs of friction against this factor.[13] The costs of friction are not,

11. Robert M. Haig, "Toward an Understanding of the Metropolis," *Quart. J. Econ.*, 40:421–423 (May 1926).

12. Richard U. Ratcliff, *Urban Land Economics* (New York: McGraw-Hill, 1949), p. 385. Neither Haig nor the later writers make clear how the minimizing of the costs of friction by the individual or the firm lead to a minimization of the aggregate. It should be noted that Ratcliff's statement is stronger than Haig's, requiring the minimizing of both components of the costs of friction. At another point, however, Ratcliff mitigates this statement to: "It is the total effect of the competition for sites to minimize the aggregate of inconvenience and frictions, as evaluated in terms of the local value systems, and hence to maximize the efficiency of the conduct of those human affairs in the community which require movement. The processes of the urban land market tend to produce the most efficient urban pattern" (p. 384). This theory is discussed further in chapter 6.

13. The literature of land economics clearly recognizes this elsewhere, but seems to ignore it when stating its basic theory of land values. It may be mentioned that Haig developed his theory from a study of manufacturing activity. The influence of von Thünen's agricultural location theory is very strong both in Haig and in later writers in land economics, who view rent as a residual after transport costs. The

by themselves, sufficient to determine location, unless changes in the volume of sales are themselves somehow considered to be "costs of friction." More generally, the minimizing of certain costs, such as the costs of friction, is a valid criterion for location only in cases where revenue and all other costs are constant, as will be shown in chapter 3.

Haig gives some consideration to residential land:

In choosing a residence purely as a consumption proposition one buys accessibility precisely as one buys clothes or food. He considers how much he wants the contacts furnished by the central location, weighing the "costs of friction" involved—the various possible combinations of site rent, time value, and transport costs; he compares this want with his other desires and his resources, and he fits into his scale of consumption and buys.[14]

The neglect of any consideration of size of site greatly weakens this statement. Whatever the size of the lot on which a residence stands, the consumer can greatly reduce his "costs of friction" by buying a smaller site, thus reducing the component "site rent." If the only criteria for residential location are accessibility to the center and the minimizing of the costs of friction, and considerations

point of view is illustrated in Ratcliff's account of the location decision: "Each activity seeks to minimize the disutilities and costs of friction by locating where its transportation costs are at a minimum. Each must be willing to pay site rent up to an amount which, added to transportation costs, is just less than the total transportation costs plus site rent for alternative locations" ("Efficiency and the Location of Urban Activities," in *The Metropolis in Modern Life*, R. M. Fisher, ed. [New York: Doubleday, 1955], p. 123). See, however, chapter 3 for a review of E. Chamberlin's pointed objections to the uncritical application of agricultural rent theory to urban values.

14. Haig, in *Quart. J. Econ.*, 40:423. Ratcliff states: "In the case of residential use . . . the convenience of the householder is the determinant of economic rent" (*Urban Land Economics*, p. 375). According to Ely and Wehrwein: "Some land is not a factor of production but is a consumption good, such as owner-occupied residential lots and recreation land. Here the value is almost all amenity value. In this case direct competition for the land—or supply or demand—sets the price" (*Land Economics*, p. 121). Note also that the definition of "costs of friction" has lost some of its clarity by the inclusion of "time value" as one of these costs. Ratcliff, *Urban Land Economics*, p. 372, also allows for the "disutilities of travel." Ely and Wehrwein, after quoting Haig, state: "Accessibility is a substitute for transportation; both have to be paid for, the former in the rent or value of land, the latter in time, inconvenience, and the cost of conveyance." (*Land Economics*, p. 138). Lowdon Wingo (see note 26 for full reference) has recently included "time value" in transport costs by attributing a dollar value to commuting time. He does not take into account, however, other "disutilities of travel" such as inconvenience, discomfort, or anxiety.

of the size of the site are excluded, all residence would be clustered around the center of the city at a very high density.[15]

The Ecologists

Parallel to the development of the literature in land economics there has developed a literature in human ecology which also concerns itself with urban land values. In a seminal book in this discipline, Park and Burgess state: "Land values are the chief determining influence in the segregation of local areas and in the determination of the uses to which an area is put."[16] While the two disciplines have influenced each other, they have remained distinct, the land economists relating primarily to economics and city planning, and the ecologists to sociology.

The ecologists view land values as a result of a bidding process by potential users, by which the pattern of location of land uses in the city is determined.[17] While their view of the process does not differ in essence from that of other writers, because of their sociological background they are greatly interested in residential location. According to Hawley, "Familial units are distributed with references [sic] to land values, the locations of other types of units, and the time and cost of transportation to centers of activity ... The influences of the three factors are combined in a single measure, namely, rental value for residential use." Hawley summarizes a generally held theory of land values in relation to residential location:

The residential property on high priced land is usually in a deteriorated condition, for since it is close to business and industrial areas it is being

15. Other writers of this school occasionally recognize the importance of the size of the site: "in urban [land] utilitization ... location and standing room are the services in demand" (H. B. Dorau and A. G. Hinman, *Urban Land Economics* [New York: Macmillan, 1928], p. 488). However, they do not develop the implications of this statement. Bloom considers size of site under "imperfections in urban land markets" (*Economic Criteria*, pp. 105ff.), but not in the "perfect" model.

16. Robert E. Park and Ernest W. Burgess (eds.), *The City* (Chicago: University of Chicago Press, 1925), p. 203. It is interesting that Haig dissociates himself from the ecologists. After recording this same quotation, he asked: "But is [it] not the uses which determine land values rather than vice versa?" (in *Quart. J. Econ.*, 40:405, fn. 4); but also see note 17.

17. For instance, James A. Quinn states: "Land values ... affect, as well as reflect, the struggle for location within the metropolis" (*Human Ecology* [New York: Prentice-Hall, 1950], p. 449). See also R. D. McKenzie, *The Metropolitan Community* (New York: McGraw-Hill, 1933).

held speculatively in anticipation of its acquisition by more intensive and therefore more remunerative land use. In view of that probability owners of such property are not disposed to spend heavily for maintenance or to engage in new residential construction. Hence the property can command a relatively low rent for family use. Moreover its proximity to various objectionable uses and its distance from family amenities also contribute to low residential values. Its accessibility, however, tends to counter the depressing effects on rents of deterioration and nearness to undesirable conditions. Conversely, new residential structures appear on low-value lands, lands that have few if any alternative uses. Since the buildings are newer and presumably better equipped for family use than those found on high-priced land, they can command a higher rent. Their protection by distance from objectionable land uses and their access to the services and utilities family life requires also favor a high rental charge. But again, the tendency to high rental valuation is minimized somewhat by the lowered general accessibility to places of employment and specialized service that greater distance involves. Thus while land values, in the main, grade downward with distance from concentrations of associational units, rental values for residential buildings grade upward. That is, rental values for residential property tend to vary inversely with land values.[18]

The paradox of low-income families living on high priced land while wealthier families live on cheaper land is explained in Hawley's theory in terms of a process over time in a growing city— or, in one that is expected to grow. Growth or its expectation is implicit in the behavior attributed to the speculators and in the expanding area which results from the continuous addition of new houses to the periphery. If new houses are built in the periphery, there must be growth of population or there would be an increasing vacancy rate in the central area of the city. It must be mentioned, however, that there is no evidence that speculators play the major role that the theory assigns them.[19] On the other hand, it will be

18. Amos H. Hawley, *Human Ecology* (New York: Ronald Press, 1950), pp. 280, 281. Quinn, however, appears to contradict the latter part of this statement: "The higher cost of land in a better residence subdivision prevents its purchase by most families of low income" (*Human Ecology*, p. 449), implying that the land occupied by low-income families is cheaper. The neglect of the size of the site is the source of confusion. The higher-income families may occupy land which is cheaper per unit of surface, but their lots may be considerably bigger, so that the total cost is greater. Ignoring the size of the site leads to frequent confusion in the literature between price per unit of land (square feet) and the value of the site (price times the quantity of land).

19. The evidence is that investment in low-income housing in central areas is very profitable. A study in central Boston showed net rates of return on investment of between 12.3 per cent and 35.2 per cent (August Nakagawa, "The 'Profitability'

shown in chapter 6 that, when the size of the site is considered explicitly, the paradox may be explained in terms of a static model as a result of the bidding process, without recourse to speculators, population growth, or the deterioration of houses. This, of course, does not disprove Hawley's theory. The model to be presented here is an alternative or a complementary theory, which may be preferable for its economy of assumptions.

The theory of minimum costs of friction appears in ecological literature, but in a modified form. The determination of location by land values has been vigorously attacked by Walter Firey, who assigns greater importance to the role of "sentiment."[20] Partly as a result of Firey's criticism, the theory has been generalized to include noneconomic factors:

Hypothesis of minimum costs . . . Ecological units tend to distribute themselves throughout an area so that the total costs of gaining maximum satisfaction in adjusting population to environment (including other men) are reduced to the minimum . . . As used in this hypothesis, the concept of cost has a very broad meaning. It includes much more than economic costs. Negatively it includes dangers encountered and disagreeable experiences undergone. It embraces whatever of value is given up or is enjoyed in lesser degree in obtaining any given pattern of adjustment. [A footnote to this passage adds:] The preceding hypotheses would not be correct except when cost is broadly defined.[21]

This broader statement explicitly denies the theory as expressed by the land economists, though it is not clear whether the rejection is based on the inclusion of noneconomic variables or whether it rejects the land economists' theory on its own terms. At any rate, the ecological theory as stated above can be neither proved nor disproved, and carries the analysis to a realm beyond the scope of the land economists or of the theory which will be presented in these pages.

---

of Slums," *Synthesis*, April 1957, p. 45). See also, Metropolitan Housing and Planning Council of Chicago, *The Road Back—The Slums* (Chicago, 1954) and Chester Rapkin, *The Real Estate Market in an Urban Renewal Area* (New York City Planning Commission, 1959), p. 120. When such profits are to be had, speculation seems superfluous.

20. Walter Firey, *Land Uses in Central Boston* (Cambridge, Mass.: Harvard University Press, 1947).

21. Quinn, *Human Ecology*, p. 282.

Other Theories

Another large body of literature has been devoted to the imperfections of the land market and to institutional factors, dealing with such matters as the very imperfect knowledge of the market by buyers and sellers, the legal complexities of the ownership and occupancy of land, the effects of zoning and taxation, and the permanence of structures, which tie down the land for long periods of time to given uses and intensities of use. R. Turvey states:

If the determinants of the equilibrium constellation of prices and resource-use changed infrequently or slowly, while adjustments to such changes took place relatively rapidly and without much friction, the actual pattern of prices and resource allocation would usually correspond fairly closely to the equilibrium pattern. It would thus be possible to analyse the existing state of affairs in terms of an equilibrium construction. Now so far as the long run is concerned, this is not generally the case with urban property, because the great durability of buildings makes urban change a very slow process and one that is never completed.

If the conditions were different and buildings had very short lives, the actual shape and form of a town would be close to its equilibrium pattern . . . But since this is not the case, since most towns are not in equilibrium, it is impossible to present a comparative static analysis which will explain the layout of towns and the pattern of buildings; the determining background conditions are insufficiently stationary in relation to the durability of buildings. In other words, each town must be examined separately and historically.

*   *   *

[The] supposed "physical" division of value into site and building values has no analytical value, and is meaningless except in long-run stationary equilibrium.[22]

In short, Turvey's opinion is that an equilibrium model of urban land uses would be worth little because the value of land is of minor importance—even if the concept were valid. There is, however, only inductive evidence as to the relative importance of land values, and the active rate of construction in downtown Manhattan and other cities, the conversion of dwellings to greater densities, and the movement and succession of activities in the urban scene may be interpreted as evidence of the importance of the value of the site in the determination of the type and intensity of land uses. There is,

22. Ralph Turvey, *The Economics of Real Property: An Analysis of Property Values and Patterns of Use* (London: Allen & Unwin, 1957), pp. 22–23, 47–48.

moreover, a strange anomaly to the discussion of imperfections of the market: namely that there is no explicit model of the "perfect" market to which these imperfections would apply. While the bidding process for land is generally accepted, the implications of this process have not been traced to a market solution, with the possible exception of the "minimum costs of friction" theory. This theory can be shown to be meaningless in one interpretation and can be disproven in another (see chapter 6).

In an interesting series of articles, Paul F. Wendt has taken issue with what he terms the "Haig-Ely-Dorau-Ratcliff hypothesis." Among the points raised is that of "price elasticities of demand and supply schedules for urban sites," though Wendt seems to be referring to the number of sites rather than to their size. Wendt criticizes many of the simplifying assumptions (as well as the conclusions) of Haig and his disciples, among them those of a single center to the city and the importance of transport costs. He offers the following theoretical model:

$$"V = \frac{f_x(P, Y, S, P_u, PI) - \sum (T + O_c + I_{im} + D_{im})}{f_x(i, R, C_g)}$$

where

$V = $ [aggregate] value of urban land
$f_x = $ expectations
$P = $ population

$Y = $ average income

$S = $ supply of competitive land
$P_u = $ competitive pull of area
$PI = $ public investment

$T = $ local taxes
$O_c = $ operative costs
$I_{im} = $ interest on improvements
$D_{im} = $ depreciation on improvements
$i = $ interest rates
$R = $ investment risk
$C_g = $ capital gain possibility."[23]

---

23. Paul F. Wendt, "Theory of Urban Land Values," *Journal of Land Economics*, 33:228–240 (August 1957); "Urban Land Value Trends," *The Appraisal Journal*, 26:254–269 (April 1958); "Economic Growth and Urban Land Values," *The Appraisal Journal*, 26:427–443 (July 1958). See also R. U. Ratcliff's rejoinder, "Commentary: On Wendt's Theory of Land Values," *Journal of Land Economics*, 33:360–362 (November 1957). The first two quotations are from the first of these articles, pp. 236–239. The value function appears in the third article, p. 427; a slightly different formulation appears on p. 235 of the first article.

In spite of its semimathematical formulation, this theory has not been precised sufficiently (except as to the direction of the effect of the variables) to justify detailed commentary here. Moreover, the majority of Wendt's variables will not be considered in the model to be presented in these pages, and those shared by both models are defined in different ways. For instance, in Wendt's model there appears "S = supply of competitive land," which is presumably a single quantity. The closest equivalent to this in our model will be a function describing the quantity of land available by geographic position. The integral of this function, in contrast to Wendt's finite stock of land, will have no upper limit. This will permit the economic determination of a "supply of competitive land" within the model, as well as the differentiation of land by its location. A more general problem in relating Wendt's theory to those he criticizes and that to be presented here is that Wendt's theory is aimed at secular and cyclical changes in aggregate land values, while the other theories are aimed at a static equilibrium and the description of variations of land values within the city at a given point in time. When these theories tend to analyze changes in aggregate land values, they do so by comparative statics.

Beckman's theory of residential land values is in many respects similar to that which will be presented in subsequent chapters. Beckman's mathematical model is aimed exclusively at residential land values, and, far from being neglected, the size of the site is the key variable of the model. One of the two explicit assumptions is that "every household chooses its residential location so as to maximize the amount of living space that it can occupy for its housing expenditure." The other explicit assumption is that "average expenditure on residence plus commuting of a household is a well defined function of income."[24] These assumptions imply that the time and bother of commuting do not, as such, affect location decisions. Given very little else than these simple assumptions, and some fairly strong assumptions about a consumption function and a linear commuting-costs function, Beckman arrives at a market solution of rent and residential densities, such that the wealthier families settle on the periphery of the city. While he does

24. Martin J. Beckman, "On the Distribution of Rent and Residential Density in Cities," paper presented at the Inter-departmental Seminar on Mathematical Applications in the Social Sciences, at Yale University, February 7, 1957 (mimeograph).

not, in his very brief paper, consider such matters as supply and demand prices or the bargaining positions of the various parties, his approach may be considered to some extent as a special case of the theory to be presented in the remaining chapters of this work.[25]

Most recently, L. Wingo has combined a theoretical analysis of traffic flows and the theories of the land economists in an explicit mathematical model of the residential land market.[26] Rents and transport costs are viewed as complementary, their sum being equal to a constant equal to the transport costs to the most distant residential location occupied. Transport costs, however, include the value of commuting time in dollars, determined by the marginal value of leisure time, though no allowance is made for the liking or disliking of the travel situation. Thus, Wingo's analysis retains and even makes stronger Haig's view of the complementarity of rent and transport costs in the urban case, in perfect parallel to von Thünen's agricultural model. As Beckman, Wingo allows the importance of the size of the site, and uses a consumption function of quantity of land with price, and finds the equilibrium level of the market through the balancing of supply and demand quantities. His analysis broadly parallels that presented in the following chapters and is presented in summary in appendix E, where the crucial points of divergence are also noted.

D. Approach and Basic Definitions

A simplifying approach will be used in these pages to develop a model of urban land values and land uses. The city is viewed as if it were located on a featureless plain, on which all land is of equal quality, ready for use without further improvements, and freely bought and sold. Both buyers and sellers will be assumed to have perfect knowledge of the market and to be unhampered by legal or

25. This theory is incorporated explicitly into the more general theory to be presented here in my doctoral dissertation, "A Model of the Urban Land Market: Location and Densities of Dwellings and Businesses," University of Pennsylvania, 1960. See particularly fn. to p. 64; illustrations on p. 65; and fn. 46 to p. 23.

26. Lowdon Wingo, Jr., *Transportation and Urban Land* (Washington, D.C.: Resources for the Future, 1961). Mr. Wingo's and my own work were carried out simultaneously and independently, neither of us aware of the other's activity. It would be necessary to devote excessive space to analyze fully the similarities and divergences between the two theories. Therefore, reference to Mr. Wingo's work will be limited to some notes and appendix E.

social restraints. Those selling land will be assumed to wish to maximize their total revenue. Those buying land will be assumed to wish to maximize profits or satisfaction, according to whether they are firms or consumers. The analysis will begin with a formal analysis of individual equilibrium of the consumer and the firm in terms of traditional substitution theory. From the analysis of individual equilibrium, we shall proceed to a derivation of market equilibrium, such that demand and supply prices and quantities are equal and the market is cleared. The market solution will include both urban and agricultural land uses in a unified theory. In the concluding chapter some complications will be introduced into the model.

Price

To avoid the thorny definitional problems that abound in the theory of rent, the emphasis will be on the process by which the value of land is determined rather than on the nature of this value. The various potential users will bid for land, and landlords will sell or rent the land to the highest bidder. Thus, the patterns of land uses and land values will be mutually determining. We shall follow Ratcliff in the use of the term:

It will be convenient to use the term "price" in its generic sense and to include under this term the market expressions of contract rent, sales price, and cost of ownership. These three values tend toward equivalence and move together, though with unevenness. Sales price, the price that a buyer is willing to pay after considering alternatives, represents the present or discounted value of future rental values. The cost of ownership is a function of both contract rent and sales price; the owner must recognize a cost of occupancy that is at least as great as the rental income he might otherwise be receiving if he were to rent out his property, and no smaller than the total of interest on the investment, taxes, maintenance, and depreciation, which total, in the long run, is in balance with rental value.[27]

In other words, the term "price" will be used for the amount of money the occupant pays or would pay to the landlord for the right to the use of a unit of land (for example, a square foot or an acre) for a given period of time. Thus, the price of land times the quantity of land in a site represents the payment for the use of the site.

27. Ratcliff, *Urban Land Economics,* pp. 347–348.

Size of the Site

The size of the site presents no conceptual problem when there is a single occupant: it is so many square feet of land.[28] However, when there are several occupants, as in the case of an apartment house, it is convenient to view the occupant of each apartment as occupying a fraction of the site. In this view, then, the two occupants of a duplex house will be regarded as occupying one-half of the site each. The same approach will be employed for profit-making firms. In this case, however, the ground floor of a building is very often more valuable than higher floors, particularly for retail purposes and personal services. While we shall not consider this element of vertical location, each tenant may be viewed as paying some fraction of the ground rent, and the sum of these parts will add to the total rent of the site. Each tenant will be viewed as occupying the same fraction of the site as the fraction of the rent he pays.

The Featureless Plain

Throughout the analysis in this work, with the exception of a part of the last chapter, we shall assume that the city sits on a featureless plain. This plain may contain lakes, or reserved land such as cemeteries, which are holes on the surface of the plain. In this sense our featureless plain is not featureless. What it does not have are such features as hills, low land, beautiful views, social cachet, or pleasant breezes. These are undoubtedly important, but no way has been found to incorporate them into the type of theory that will be presented. However, the reader may perhaps prefer to think of the featureless plain not as a simple grey surface, but rather as an average of cities, where an elevation in one city may be matched by a depression in another, or the social disesteem of an area in this city is compensated by the historic associations of a matching area in that city. These incidents of such importance in the particular case are distractions when one considers the general case in order to understand the process and structure of urban areas.

28. It should be noted that in real estate practice the size of the lot is often measured in terms of "front feet" (street frontage). The areal measure will be preferred here as more suitable for general purposes than the linear for the measurement of an area. However, the model to be presented could be adapted to the linear measure.

2

Equilibrium of the Household

A. Introduction

An individual who arrives in a city and wishes to buy some land to live upon will be faced with the double decision of how large a lot he should purchase and how close to the center of the city he should settle. In reality he would also consider the apparent character and racial composition of the neighborhood, the quality of the schools in the vicinity, how far away he would be from any relatives he might have in the city, and a thousand other factors. However, the individual in question is an "economic man," defined and simplified in a way such that we can handle the analysis of his decision-making.[1] He merely wishes to maximize his satisfaction by owning and consuming the goods he likes and avoiding those he dislikes. Moreover, an individual is in reality a family which may contain several members. Their decisions may be reached in a family council or be the responsibility of a single member. We are not concerned with how these tastes are formed, but simply with what they are. Given these tastes, this simplified family will spend whatever money it has available in maximizing its satisfaction.

The city in which the individual arrives is a simplified city. It lies on a featureless plain, and transportation is possible in all directions. All employment and all goods and services are available only at the center of the city. Land is bought and sold by free contract, without any institutional restraints and without having its character fixed by any structures existing upon the ground. Municipal services and

---

1. Purposeful simplification for analysis is so much the rule and its advantages and disadvantages have been discussed so thoroughly that further discussion of it here is unnecessary. However, on the particular issue of residential location and urban structure, an interesting polemic was started by Walter Firey (*Land Uses in Central Boston*, chap. 1), who attacked the simplifications of human ecologists. A reply from this group may be found in Amos Hawley, *Human Ecology*, pp. 179–180, 286.

tax rates are uniform throughout the city. The individual knows the price of land at every location, and, from his point of view, this is a given fact, not affected by his decisions. *P given*

In this chapter we shall find how much land and where such an individual would buy in such a city. Finding these things constitutes the equilibrium solution for the individual. It will be found in this chapter by means of classical consumer equilibrium theory, though the unusual nature of the problem will call forth unexpected turns from the theory. However, though classical theory is satisfactory for the description of individual equilibrium, it does not enable us in this case to aggregate individuals to arrive at a market solution without a radical reformulation. In order to understand this reformulation, the classical solution must be thoroughly grasped. It will be explored in detail in the following pages, first diagrammatically, and later mathematically. For the reader who is not thoroughly familiar with the general case of the classical consumer equilibrium theory, its essentials, both in the diagrammatic and the mathematical versions, are presented in appendix D.

B. DIAGRAMMATIC SOLUTION OF INDIVIDUAL EQUILIBRIUM

To describe individual equilibrium diagrammatically, we must represent graphically both all of the alternatives open to the individual and his pattern of preferences. By joining these two diagrams, we can observe which of the opportunities open to the individual he will choose.

Opportunities Open to the Individual

The individual has at his disposal a certain income which he may spend as he wishes. Out of this income he must pay for his land costs, his commuting costs and for all other goods and services (including savings). We wish to describe diagrammatically all of the choices open to the consumer, subject to the restriction of his budget. This restriction may be expressed thus:

Individual's income
= land costs + commuting costs + all other expenditures

First let us examine his expenditures for all goods and services excepting land and commuting costs. The individual may buy greater or smaller quantities of a wide variety of goods. We may denominate the quantity of each good he purchases by $z_1, z_2, \ldots, z_n$, for each of n goods. If the prices of these n goods are $p_1, p_2, \ldots, p_n$, then the expenditure by the individual for any good z_i will be equal to the price of that good times the quantity of the good purchased: $p_i z_i$. His total expenditure for the goods and services in this category will be:

$$p_1 z_1 + p_2 z_2 + \cdots + p_n z_n.$$

However, for the sake of simplicity we shall group all these various goods and services into one composite good, z. The price of this composite good will be a price index, p_z. The expenditure on all goods and services other than land or commuting costs will be $p_z z$.

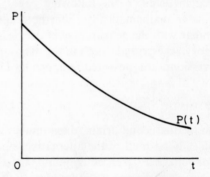

FIGURE 1. Diagrammatic structure of land prices

This simplification will not affect the logic of the subsequent analysis. As an alternative, z may be considered to be money, and p_z may be regarded as unity.

Second, let us examine the individual's expenditures on land. From the point of view of the individual, a price structure is given which specifies a price for land at every location. This price structure is represented by curve $P(t)$ in Figure 1. Price of land, P, varies with distance from the center of the city, t.[2] By expressing the price

2. It will be assumed here that the price of land decreases with increasing distance from the center of the city. Below it will be seen that this is a requirement for the existence of both individual and market equilibrium as well as essentially true for most cities.

structure in this manner, it is clear that when a location is chosen, a given price of land is implied.

However, in purchasing land the consumer not only chooses a location but must also decide upon the quantity of land he will acquire. We shall represent this quantity by the letter q. The expenditure on land will be equal to the price of land times the quantity purchased: $P(t)q$.

Thirdly, we wish to consider commuting costs. These will increase with increasing distance from the center of the city. We shall represent these costs by the function $k(t)$ where t corresponds to the same location as in $P(t)$.

We can now write the budget equation that will contain all of the choices open to a person of income y:

(2:1) $$y = p_z z + P(t)q + k(t)$$

where y: income;

p_z: price of the composite good;

z: quantity of the composite good;

$P(t)$: price of land at distance t from the center of the city;

q: quantity of land;

$k(t)$: commuting costs to distance t;

t: distance from the center of the city.

Equation (2:1) contains within it all the possible alternative ways in which the individual may spend his money. We shall now diagram this function. This can be done in a 3-dimensional set of co-ordinates in terms of the variables z, q, and t. These three variables are the determining ones since income (y) and the price of the composite good (p_z) are given, and the price of land, $P(t)$, and commuting costs, $k(t)$, are functions in terms of t. We shall obtain a 3-dimensional surface that will represent all of the alternatives open to the consumer, and this surface will be called the *locus of opportunities*. Every point on the surface is a possible alternative open to the consumer; every point not on the surface is not a possible alternative.[3] To describe the locus of opportunities surface we shall

3. The locus of opportunities is a generalization of the budget or price line of the usual case. Both describe all of the choices available given a certain income. However, while the budget line considers choices among goods at definite prices, in this case the locus of opportunities considers a good, q, of varying price, $P(t)$, and a good, t, which has no price but determines the price of good q and commuting costs, $k(t)$. Though the budget line is therefore a special case of the locus of opportunities, they both serve the same analytical function.

consider sections through it by holding each of the three variables constant in succession and observing the variations of the other two.

First, let us fix t at any distance $t = t_0$. The individual can now choose between varying quantities of land, q, and the composite good, z, while distance is for the moment fixed at t_0. Distance being fixed, so are price of land, at $P(t_0)$, and commuting costs, at $k(t_0)$. Equation (2:1) becomes

$$y = p_z z + P(t_0)q + k(t_0),$$

which may be rewritten as

$$q = \frac{y - k(t_0)}{P(t_0)} - \frac{p_z}{P(t_0)} z.$$

This is a linear equation, with a slope equal to the negative of the ratio of the prices of the two goods. Its intercepts are $q = 0$, $z = [y - k(t_0)]/p_z$, and $z = 0$, $q = [y - k(t_0)]/P(t_0)$. It is shown in Figure 2.

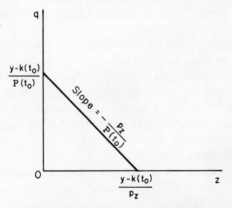

FIGURE 2. Locus of opportunities between q and z, when t is constant at t_0

Now let us hold the composite good constant at $z = z_0$, and allow q and t to vary. Equation (2:1) becomes

$$y = p_z z_0 + P(t)q + k(t),$$

which may be rewritten as

$$q = \frac{y - p_z z_0 - k(t)}{P(t)}.$$

This is not a simple linear equation. The price of land, $P(t)$, in the denominator, decreases with increasing distance from the center of the city. Therefore the quantity of land that may be bought, q, increases with distance, since land is becoming cheaper. On the other hand, distance enters into the numerator in the form of commuting costs, $k(t)$. As distance increases, so do commuting costs, and consequently the amount of land that may be purchased decreases. Thus, distance acts in opposing directions upon the quantity of land. The resulting curve is shown in Figure 3. The curve of q on t rises up to the point at which marginal increases in commuting costs are equal to the savings realized from the decreasing price of land. Thereafter, the amount of land that may be

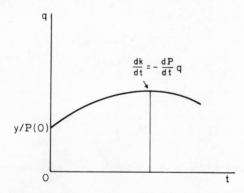

FIGURE 3. Locus of opportunities between q and t, when z is constant at z_0

bought with increasing distance decreases. (See appendix F, note 1 for the formal derivation of the turning point of the curve.)

And lastly, let us hold q constant at q_0 and allow t and z to vary. Equation (2:1) becomes

$$y = p_z z + P(t)q_0 + k(t),$$

which may be rewritten as

$$z = \frac{y - P(t)q_0 - k(t)}{p_z}.$$

The denominator of the fraction is a constant, p_z. The numerator, on the other hand, contains two expressions in terms of t. The first,

$P(t)q_0$, will cause z to increase with t since $P(t)$ will be decreasing and the expression is preceded by a negative sign. The second, $k(t)$, also preceded by a minus sign, increases with t and therefore causes z to decrease. The resulting curve is shown in Figure 4. These two opposing effects of distance will cause the amount of the composite good to increase as long as the savings resulting from cheaper land exceed the increases in commuting costs, and the amount of the composite good will decrease when increases in commuting costs exceed the savings resulting from cheaper land. (See appendix F, note 2 for the formal derivation of the turning point of the curve.)

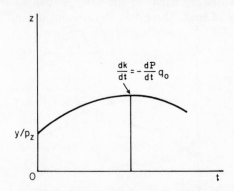

FIGURE 4. Locus of opportunities between z and t, when q is constant at q_0

Now that we have three sections through the locus of opportunities surface, we may draw it in three dimensions. This has been done in Figure 5. A section parallel to the q–z plane would yield a curve corresponding to that of Figure 2. A section parallel to the q–t plane would yield a curve corresponding to Figure 3. And a section parallel to the z–t plane will yield a curve corresponding to that of Figure 4.[4] The shell-like surface contains all of the combinations of land (q), the composite good (z), and distance (t) open to the consumer, and his equilibrium solution must be a point on this surface.[5] It should be noted that a higher income would have

4. At $q = 0$, such a section would show z decreasing monotonically with increases in t. This, of course is a special case of the typical humped curve, where the high point of the curve occurs at $t = 0$.

5. The surface bounded by dashed lines corresponds to the locus of opportunities that would obtain if there were no commuting costs. It is, of course, higher than the surface for the case with costs of commuting, since these costs are equivalent to

yielded a locus of opportunities surface of the same shape but above the one in Figure 5, while a lower income would have yielded one below it.

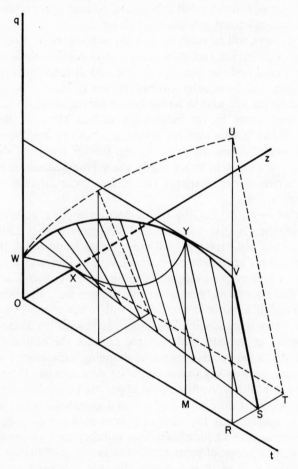

FIGURE 5. Locus of opportunities surface

reductions in income or reduced purchasing power. As one instance, the quantity of land $q = RV$ bought where there are commuting costs (and no z is purchased) will be $[y - k(R)]/P(R)$, while the quantity of land $q = RV$ that would be bought if there were no commuting costs would be $y/P(R)$. The quantity of land lost to commuting expenses is $k(R)/P(R)$.

Preferences of the Individual

We now wish to map the individual's preferences. When the mapping of preferences is joined with the mapping of opportunities, individual equilibrium will correspond to that opportunity which yields the individual greatest satisfaction.

Preferences will be mapped through *indifference surfaces*. In this case an indifference surface will be a set of combinations of quantities of land and the composite good and distance, such that the individual will be equally satisfied by any of these combinations. Hence, he may be said to be indifferent among all of the combinations represented by the indifference surface. However, the usual shape of indifference surfaces is that of a bowl propped up against the corner of a box. In this case, the strange nature of the good distance will result in an unusually shaped indifference surface. We shall arrive at the shape of the surface by examining sections through it.

Let us begin by holding the composite good, z, constant, and allowing the quantity of land, q, and distance, t, to vary. Land q is a good of the ordinary type. All other things being equal, the individual will prefer to have more than less of it; that is to say, he will prefer to have ample living space and not to be crowded. Distance, t, on the other hand, is unusual. We assume that, all other things being equal, a rational individual will prefer a more accessible location to a less accessible one. Since t represents the distance from the center of the city, and thus the distance the individual must commute to the principal place of shopping, amusement, and employment, we may say that accessibility decreases as t increases. In other words, the individual would prefer t to be smaller rather than larger, so that t may be thought of as a good with negative utility (that is, satisfaction). Increases in t produce dissatisfaction.

Given these two goods, then, how will they vary while maintaining a constant level of satisfaction? Given any combination of land and distance, a small increase in distance will produce dissatisfaction, and will have to be compensated for by a small increase in the quantity of land for satisfaction to remain the same. The indifference curve, between land and distance, therefore, will be a rising curve, q increasing with t, as in Figure 6. Had we plotted accessibility rather than distance against land, we would have obtained a downward sloping indifference curve of the usual shape.

However, since distance can be measured directly, while accessibility implies some subjective pattern of preference (or nuisance value of distance) which may vary from one individual to another, it is better for our purposes to use distance as the variable and to let the shape of the indifference curves take care of the relation between distance and accessibility.

In spite of the direction of the slope of this indifference curve, it remains true, as in the usual case, that lower curves will represent less satisfaction (less land at the same distance, or more distance for

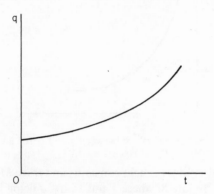

FIGURE 6. Indifference curve between q and t, for a constant z_0

the same quantity of land) and higher curves greater satisfaction. It also remains true that curves of this family will not cross.

Now let us hold distance constant at $t = t_0$ and observe the variations between land and the composite good. Given any combination of q and z, a small decrease in one will have to be compensated by a small increase of the other for satisfaction to remain constant. This is the usual type of indifference curve, as in Figure 7. The curve will not only slope downward to the right, but it will also be convex toward the origin, by reason of the diminishing marginal utility of the goods.

Finally, let us hold the quantity of land constant at $q = q_0$ and allow distance and the composite good to vary. A small increase in distance increases the nuisance of commuting, and requires a small increase in the quantity of the composite good for satisfaction to remain constant. There will result a curve as in Figure 8, sloping upward to the right.

We can now draw an indifference surface in these three dimensions, z, q, and t, by combining these three sections. Figure 9 shows such a surface. Figure 10 shows the same surface; the trace XY on plane A corresponds to Figure 6 above, where q and t vary and z is held constant; trace $QRST$ on plane B corresponds to Figure 7,

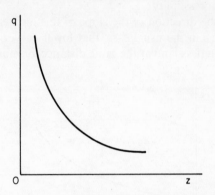

FIGURE 7. Indifference curve between q and z, for a constant t_0

where q and z vary and t is held constant; and trace MN on plane C corresponds to Figure 8, where z and t vary, q being held constant.

The indifference surface shown in Figure 9 represents all of the combinations of the three goods, z, q, and t, which yield the same level of satisfaction to the individual. Combinations of these goods yielding different levels of satisfaction would be represented by

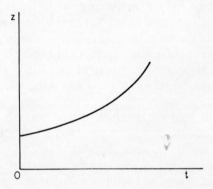

FIGURE 8. Indifference curve between z and t, for a constant q_0

similarly shaped surfaces, higher ones for more satisfaction and lower ones for less.

Equilibrium of the Individual

We now have a description of the individual's preferences in the indifference surfaces mapping, and a description of all of the opportunities open to the individual in the locus of opportunities surface. If we join the two mappings, we can see which of the available

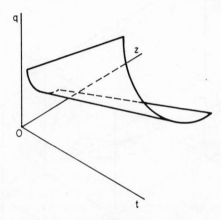

FIGURE 9. An indifference surface

opportunities the individual will prefer. This will be the combination of goods represented by the point at which the locus of opportunities surface touches the highest (that is, most satisfactory) of the indifference surfaces with which it comes in contact. If the point be z_i, q_i, t_i, the individual will purchase quantity z_i of the composite good at price p_z, he will occupy q_i land at distance t_i from the center of the city, for which he pays a price $P(t_i)$, and he will spend $k(t_i)$ on commuting costs.

By examining carefully the shape of the indifference and of the locus of opportunities surfaces, it becomes clear that the point of equilibrium must lie within the portion of the locus of opportunities (Figure 5) bounded by the curves WX, XY, and YW. At the equilibrium point, the locus of opportunities and the indifference surface must be tangent to each other, since both are smooth surfaces touching at a point. Therefore the two surfaces must be parallel at that point. The indifference surface (see Figure 9) is shaped like a trough, and it moves up and away from the *t*-axis. The locus of opportunities, however, moves up and away from the *t*-axis only over the portion *W X Y*. Therefore tangency between the curves and individual equilibrium are possible only in this section.

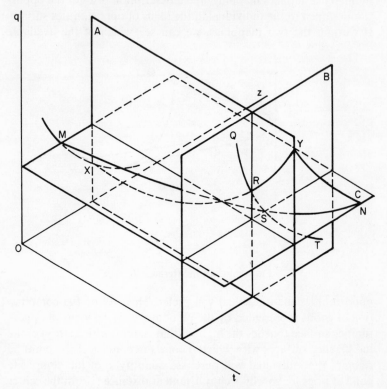

FIGURE 10. Sections through an indifference surface

C. MATHEMATICAL SOLUTION OF INDIVIDUAL EQUILIBRIUM

The mathematical solution of individual equilibrium parallels the diagrammatic solution but is at once more general and more compact. We may start with the proposition that the individual has a given income, *y*, which he may spend as he pleases between *z* and *q*, after he pays the commuting costs $k(t)$ attendant to his location.

This proposition is expressed in the *budget balance* equation

(2:1) $$y = p_z z + P(t)q + k(t).$$

As before, we assume that we are given the price of the composite good p_z and the functions of the cost of land with distance, $P(t)$, and of commuting costs with distance, $k(t)$. The problem consists of finding the possible set of z, q, and t which both satisfies the budget balance equation (which corresponds to the locus of opportunities surface) and yields the individual the greatest satisfaction.

The satisfaction of the individual is given in the function

(2:2) $$u = u(z, q, t),$$

called the utility function. Given a set of values z_0, q_0, t_0, we find u_0 by means of this function. For another set z_i, q_i, t_i, we would find u_i. Then, if u_i is greater than u_0, we may say that the set z_i, q_i, t_i is preferable to the set z_0, q_0, t_0.[6]

The individual will try to maximize his satisfaction within the restraints of his income. In other words, the problem is to discover which combination z_i, q_i, t_i that satisfies the budget balance equation (2:1) yields the highest value for u in equation (2:2). This is done by differential calculus. Differentiating the utility function (2:2) we obtain

(2:3) $$du = u_z\, dz + u_q\, dq + u_t\, dt.[7]$$

At the point at which satisfaction, u, is maximized, $du = 0$, so that

(2:4) $$du = 0 = u_z\, dz + u_q\, dq + u_t\, dt.$$

According to the conditions of maximization for multivariable functions, we can hold all variables but two constant, and the sum of the partials times the differentials of the remaining two will still equal zero. Thus, if we hold t constant so that $dt = 0$, equation (2:4) becomes

(2:5) $$du = 0 = u_z\, dz + u_q\, dq + 0.$$

6. The reader is reminded that the values of u have only ordinal properties, and that they are equivalent to the naming (in some sequence) of the indifference surfaces.

7. For convenience in notation, as is frequently done, we shall denote the partial derivative of a function with respect to a variable by the name (letter) of that function with the variable as a subscript. Thus,

$$u_z = \partial u/\partial z; \quad u_q = \partial u/\partial q; \quad u_t = \partial u/\partial t.$$

Equation (2:5) may be rewritten as

(2:6) $-dz/dq = u_q/u_z$.

If we hold q constant, so that $dq=0$, from equation (2:4) we obtain

(2:7) $du = 0 = u_z\,dz + 0 + u_t\,dt$.

Equation (2:7) may be rewritten as

(2:8) $-dz/dt = u_t/u_z$.

Now we return to the budget balance equation (2:1). Differentiating we have

(2:9) $dy = y_z\,dz + y_q\,dq + y_P\,dP + y_k\,dk$.

But y is a given constant, so that $dy=0$. As we have an explicit statement of the equation (2:1), we can find the partial derivatives. These are:

$$y_z = p_z; \quad y_q = P(t); \quad y_P = q; \quad y_k = 1.$$

Substituting these into equation (2:9), we obtain

(2:10) $0 = p_z\,dz + P(t)\,dq + q\,dP + dk$.

We can solve for dP and dk in terms of dt by the differentials of $P(t)$ and $k(t)$, so that

$$dP = (dP/dt)dt \quad \text{and} \quad dk = (dk/dt)dt.$$

Substituting these into equation (2:10), we have

$$0 = p_z\,dz + P(t)dq + q(dP/dt)dt + (dk/dt)dt,$$

which may be rewritten as

(2:11) $0 = p_z\,dz + P(t)dq + dt(q\,dP/dt + dk/dt)$.

Equation (2:11) is, of course, merely a rewriting of equation (2:9).

The rule that we may hold all variables but two constant applies to constants as well as maxima. Since y is a constant, from equation (2:11), holding first t and then q constant, we may say that

$$0 = p_z\,dz + P(t)dq + 0,$$

and $0 = p_z\,dz + 0 + dt(q\,dP/dt + dk/dt)$.

These may be rewritten as

$$(2:12) \qquad -dz/dq = P(t)/p_z,$$

$$(2:13) \qquad -dz/dt = (q\,dP/dt + dk/dt)/p_z.$$

Combining equations (2:6) and (2:8) with equations (2:12) and (2:13), we obtain

$$(2:14) \qquad u_q/u_z = P(t)/p_z \qquad \text{and}$$

$$(2:15) \qquad u_t/u_z = (q\,dP/dt + dk/dt)/p_z.$$

Equations (2:14) and (2:15), together with the budget balance equation (2:1), are three equations which, when solved simultaneously, yield the individual's optimal combinations of the three unknowns, z, q, and t.[8] Finding these unknowns constitutes the solution of the individual's equilibrium.

Interpretation of the Mathematical Solution

The interpretation of the mathematical solution is the same as that of the diagrammatic solution, though it permits greater precision. The budget balance equation (2:1) requires no explanation, since we constructed it by definition. It corresponds to the locus of opportunities of the diagrammatic solution. However, equations (2:14) and (2:15) should be examined closely.

First, let us look at the relation between the utility function and the indifference surface. The indifference surface is the locus of all combinations of goods z, q, and t which yield the same satisfaction to the individual. In terms of the utility function this means that all these combinations of z, q, and t will yield the same value for u. The marginal rates of substitution between goods (the rate at which the individual is willing to exchange small quantities of one good for small quantities of another) are represented in the diagrammatic

---

8. Strictly speaking, we do not have just three equations and three unknowns. We have seven unknowns: z, q, t, $P(t)$, dP/dt, $k(t)$, and dk/dt. The additional four equations are given by the stated functions $P(t)$ and $k(t)$ and their derivatives. This proliferation of unknowns and equations occurs if we regard the four additional unknowns as requiring numerical solution. If we view P, k, dP/dt, and dk/dt as functions in terms of t, then the three original equations are sufficient since we then have only three unknowns. The whole matter of the number of equations between three and seven depends on whether we count unknowns and equations before or after we have effected the substitutions for $P(t)$, $k(t)$, dP/dt, and dk/dt.

solution by the slope of the indifference surface. The slope is measured parallel to the plane defined by the axes of the two goods. In the mathematical solution, this slope (that is, the marginal rate of substitution) is represented by the ratio of the marginal utilities of the two goods. The marginal utility of a good is the partial derivative of utility, u, with respect to that good.

Returning now to equations (2:14) and (2:15), we note that the left-hand sides of the equations are marginal rates of substitution. The right-hand sides of the equations make statements about costs. As in the usual case in this type of analysis, these equations state that, at equilibrium, the marginal rate of substitution between two goods is equal to the ratio of their marginal costs. If they were not, the individual would not be at equilibrium since he could increase his satisfaction by acquiring more of the relatively cheaper good.

Equation (2:14) is very simple. It states that, at equilibrium, the marginal rate of substitution (u_q/u_z) between land (q) and all other goods (z) is equal to the ratio of their prices, that is, their marginal costs.

Equation (2:15) is somewhat more complicated. It states that, at equilibrium, the marginal rate of substitution (u_t/u_z) between distance (t) and the composite good (z), is equal to ($q\ dP/dt + dk/dt)/p_z$. In the denominator we recognize p_z, the price and marginal cost of z. The numerator represents the marginal cost of spatial movement. It is the change in the price of land dP/dt (as it changes with distance) times the quantity of land, q, plus the change in commuting costs, dk/dt. Thus, once again the marginal rate of substitution is equal to the ratio of the marginal costs.

We had assumed that a near location was preferred to a distant one, since commuting is generally regarded as a nuisance. This means that u_t is a marginal disutility, and has negative utility; in short, that $u_t < 0$. But we had also assumed that increases in good z had a positive utility ($u_z > 0$), and implicitly, that $p_z > 0$. It follows, therefore, that the expression $q\ dP/dt + dk/dt$ must be smaller than zero for equation (2:15) to hold.

Let us examine this expression. We can expect that $dk/dt > 0$, since commuting costs increase with the distance traveled. The value of q, the quantity of land, can certainly be no less than zero. We must conclude that dP/dt is negative, for otherwise the expression would be positive. That is to say, the individual cannot arrive at equilibrium except on a negative stretch of the curve $P(t)$.

If $P(t)$ were positively inclined—price of land increasing with distance from the center of the city—the individual would move toward the center, where he would get cheaper land and do less commuting.

There is a further conclusion. Since, for equilibrium, it is necessary that $(q \, dP/dt + dk/dt) < 0$, the individual will never settle where $-(q \, dP/dt) < dk/dt$. This is the same conclusion we arrived at diagrammatically, when we stated that the individual will only settle where the savings derived from cheaper land exceed increased commuting costs. This is the portion WXY of the locus of opportunities surface in Figure 5.

Agricultural Rent Functions and Bid Price Curves of the Urban Firm

A. INTRODUCTION

In chapter 2 we have seen how the equilibrium solution of the individual resident may be found. We now wish to arrive at a formulation of market equilibrium. However, the classical form of solution for the individual cannot be used in this case to derive the structure of demand in the market. In the usual case, from the individual solution, one may derive a miniature demand curve for that person by varying the price of the commodity. If the demand curves of all persons are aggregated, one obtains a demand curve for the market. But in this case, land and distance are so intertwined that we cannot derive such a curve.

To illustrate this point, let us examine the variations in the quantity of land bought by an individual at a given location, t_0, as the price of land, $P(t_0)$, varies. The individual must maintain his budget balanced, so that equation (2:1) must hold:

$$(2:1) \qquad y = p_z z + P(t_0)q + k(t_0).$$

The individual decides how he will spend his money between land, q, and the composite good, z, by comparing the ratio of their prices to their marginal rate of substitution in equation

$$(2:14) \qquad u_q/u_z = P(t_0)/p_z.$$

By allowing the price P at location t_0 to vary, and solving for q and z, we can obtain the demand curve, which relates q to $P(t_0)$. But this demand curve will obtain only for that individual at *that* location. Variations in distance will affect the amount of money at his disposal by affecting the commuting costs term in equation (2:1). Equally as important, since both the marginal utilities u_q and u_z in equation (2:14) are functions of z, q, and t, the marginal rate of substitution will vary as t varies. Consequently, the demand curves for the same individual will vary with his location. Since part of the problem of finding the market solution consists of finding individual locations, not knowing the locations of individuals we would not know which of their demand curves to use to build up our market demand curve.

There are difficult problems on the supply side as well. The principal one is that of defining the supply of land. While there is a fixed supply of land at any given distance from the center of the city, the total supply of land may be regarded as infinite for any practical purpose. The total supply of land, therefore, cannot be regarded as a fixed, finite quantity; rather, it must be viewed as a collection of stocks of land differentiated by their location.

These problems are similar to those encountered in the theory of agricultural rent and land use. In this chapter we shall examine a greatly simplified agricultural model to learn the method by which it handles the land market. The problem of the location of urban firms will be investigated as one that shares characteristics with the problems of both the agricultural and the residential land uses. In the light of this analysis, individual equilibrium will be restated in chapter 4 in a form that can be used to arrive at a market solution.

B. A Simple Model of Agricultural Rent and Land Use

The theory of spatial structure of agricultural production originated in 1826 in J. H. von Thünen's theory of the isolated city. Two recent and more complete statements are those by W. Isard and E. S. Dunn.[1] While this analysis can reach a very high level of complexity, the version presented here will be greatly simplified.[2]

In this type of model there is a single market at which agricultural produce can be sold, and all produce is shipped to this market. All land is on a featureless plain. Various crops may be considered, but for simplicity we shall deal with only one at first.

Let that crop be, for instance, corn. One acre of land will produce

1. Von Thünen, *Der isolierte Staat* (Hamburg, 1826); Isard, *Location and Space-Economy*; Dunn, *The Location of Agricultural Production*.
2. The principal omissions from the analysis are: (1) variations in the intensity of use, (2) variations in the costs of production with distance, (3) crop mixtures, and (4) the effects of varying fertility of land.

30 bushels of corn at a cost of $10 in labor and machinery. The price of a bushel of corn is $1 at the market, and consequently one acre's production sells for $30. If corn were produced right at the market, value would exceed costs at the rate of $20 per acre. However, corn produced at any distance from the market must pay shipping costs. If these costs are $0.05 per bushel per mile, an acre of land at 10 miles from the market would have $15 in shipping costs in addition to $10 in production costs. Since revenue remains at $30, the gap between revenue and costs is only $5. At distances greater than $13\frac{1}{3}$ miles, costs will exceed revenues, and no corn will be produced.

The gap between revenues and costs is economic rent in the technical sense and becomes rent paid to the landlord in the ordinary sense. Suppose no rent is paid. A farmer notices that the gap between costs and revenues one mile nearer the market is $1.50 per acre greater than at his location, and 2 miles nearer the market the gap is $3 per acre greater. He will bid rents for these locations up to these amounts. The competition among farmers for the more favored locations converts this gap into rent and "wipes away any surplus profit which might befall the operator at any site."[3] The farmer retains only "normal profits," which may be regarded as a form of labor costs.

The rent at any location may be calculated from the expression

$$p_c(t) = N[P_c - C - k_c(t)],$$

where $p_c(t_0)$: the rent per unit of land at a distance t_0 from the market;

N: number of units of the crop produced per unit of land;

P_c: price per unit of the crop at the market;

C: cost of producing one unit of the crop;

$k_c(t_0)$: cost of transporting one unit of the product a distance t_0 to the market.

This rent function[4] is shown as $p_c(t)$ in Figure 11. The location t_e is that location at which rent is zero. At distances greater than t_e corn could be produced only at a loss.

---

3. Isard, *Location and Space-Economy*, p. 196.

4. This is the term used by Isard and Dunn. E. M. Hoover (*Location Theory and the Shoe and Leather Industries* [Cambridge, Mass.: Harvard University Press, 1937]), prefers "rent surface," emphasizing its three-dimensional nature.

We can now compute the total production of corn. It will be

$$\text{total production} = N \cdot S(t_e).$$

The function $S(t)$ denotes how much land is bounded by a circle of radius t around the market; t_e is the most distant location at which the crop is grown. In a featureless plain, $S(t)$ would be πt^2. $S(t_e)$ represents, then, the area over which the crop is grown, and N the number of units of the crop produced per unit of area. Should the total amount of corn produced at price P_c exceed the demand at

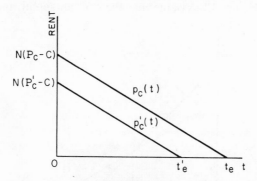

FIGURE 11. Agricultural bid rents for the same crop at two different market prices

that price, the price will drop to some lower value P_c'. There results a generally lower rent function (curve $p_c'(t)$ in Figure 11); the farthest distance at which corn would be produced would be t_e' (smaller than t_e), and the total production of corn would be reduced. Thus, through changes in the market price of the produce, the total production of the crop is brought into line with the demand for it. Rents, which are a residual, are downgraded as the price of the good drops.

This analysis has been at the level of the industry: in this case, corn-growing industry. How does it relate to the individual farmer at the level of the firm? The competition among farmers insures that all surplus profits go to the landlord in the form of rent, but at the same time it insures normal returns to the farmer whatever his location to motivate him to work his land.[5] "Thus, theoretically,

5. These normal profits are now considered as part of the costs of production, C, in the equation on page 38.

the farm operator is indifferent to the position at which he is located, provided, of course, he is within the rent-yielding hinterland. Hence, observing the adjustments of the individual agricultural entrepreneur at each possible distance from the market yields, for the given crop, a theoretically valid rent function."[6] In other words, the industry's rent function for a given market price may be viewed also as the rent a farmer would be willing to pay the landlords at each of these locations.

Let us introduce another crop, wheat, with a rent function $p_w(t)$ as shown in Figure 12. Assume that the over-all supply and demand

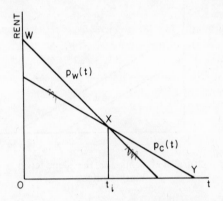

FIGURE 12. Bid rent functions for two crops

quantities are in balance. Wheat farmers can pay a higher rent for land than corn farmers in the area between the market ($t=0$) and distance t_i, and landlords will rent their land to wheat farmers in this range. On the other hand, corn producers can pay a rent higher than wheat producers at distances greater than t_i, and that land will be put into the production of corn. The function denoting the rents actually paid will be WXY. The meaning of the $p_c(t)$ curve to the left of t_i and of $p_w(t)$ to the right of that point, then, is that these are unsuccessful bids for the land rather than the rents actually paid. A distinction must be drawn between rent functions which are rents actually paid and those which represent rents someone is willing to pay. The latter type may be unsuccessful in securing the land; if

6. Isard, *Location and Space-Economy*, p. 196.

they are successful they represent actual rents. For example, the equation $p_c(t) = N[P_c - C - k_c(t)]$ represents a *bid rent function* for corn; that part of the curve to the right of t_i represents unsuccessful bids; that part to the left of t_i represents successful bids.

More crops might be added to this analysis without changing its main features. Finally, when "... it is desirable to consider each firm by itself ... each firm can be considered as an industry. More boundary variables are introduced but so are more equations to determine the variables ... Thus firm and industry are mutually consistent in the spatial framework, and in the extreme case may be considered as one and the same thing."[7]

This very brief review suffices to point to the principal means of aggregating demand for the agricultural production factor land. First, for each of the competing users (firm or industry) a family of bid rent curves is derived, each curve corresponding to a given market price for the product and to a given level of profits for the farm operator (in the agricultural model these profits are "normal" in every case). Then, taking from the family of curves for each bidder the bid rent curve that corresponds to the appropriate market price for the produce, the curves of all the potential users of land are compared at all locations, and the land at each location is assigned to the highest bidder. These highest bids, taken together, constitute the actual rent structure. However, the "appropriate market price for the produce" must be found simultaneously. This is done by establishing the price at which sufficient land and no more is secured to produce the correct amount of the produce according to the demand schedule.[8] This price identifies which curve of the family of bid rent curves should be used. This curve states the rent for land the producers of that commodity are willing to pay at various locations, given that market price for their produce.

Abstracting from the particulars of agriculture, the method reduces to: (1) for each potential user of land, a family of bid rent functions is derived, such that the user is indifferent as to his location along any *one* of these functions; (2) equilibrium price at any

---

7. *Ibid.*, p. 248. The problem is stated in the form of a system of simultaneous equations, and a general statement is found in the section "Agricultural Location Theory Embraced and Generalized," pp. 243–251. The problem of finite vs. infinite price elasticities of demand faced by the industry and the firm cannot be discussed here. However, if market price is regarded as fixed, the statement is accurate.

8. This involves either an iterative series or a simultaneous solution.

location is found by comparing the bids of the potential users and choosing the highest; and (3) equilibrium quantities of land are found by selection of the proper bid rent function for each user. In the solution, the second and third steps are interdependent and must be brought into agreement either through a simultaneous or an iterative solution.

C. Equilibrium of the Firm

Before trying to apply the general method of agriculture to residential land use, we shall examine commercial firms in the city as an intermediate problem, sharing characteristics of both. Moreover, whereas no formal theory of residential land use has been put forward in the literature, there has been some discussion of the possibility of extending the method of agricultural theory to urban commercial land uses.

Two authors who consider this possibility are E. Chamberlin and W. Isard. The latter is optimistic: "Yet it suffices to disclose the rather obvious interconnections of agricultural location theory and urban land use theory. In each, rent functions (surfaces) guide the allocating hand of the market. For both, relations to transportation facilities and systems are critical in the definition of effective economic distance."[9] Chamberlin, on the other hand, is pessimistic: "Urban rent for retailing purposes is a different sort of income from agricultural rent—in fact, although the two types are ordinarily thought of as analogous, the only resemblance between them appears to be that they are both paid for land."[10] But he goes on to say: "The rent of urban land is explained wholly, that of agricultural land partly, by the factor of location." He seems to be referring here to the differences in the fertility of land in agriculture. However, the theory of agricultural location is based almost exclusively on location: fertility differences are introduced later, as a complicating factor.[11] Both Isard and Chamberlin, then, are saying much the same thing, though they differ in their attitude.

9. Isard, *Location and Space-Economy*, p. 205.
10. E. Chamberlin, *The Theory of Monopolistic Competition* (6th ed.; Cambridge, Mass.: Harvard University Press, 1950), p. 266.
11. This is true only of modern post-von Thünen theorists. The earlier theorists, from Ricardo on, concentrated principally on fertility differentials, to the neglect of the location factor.

Chamberlin mentions some further differences between agriculture and urban retailing. He points out that the farmer pays for the productive ability, the retailer for the selling ability of land; that the farmer's site is at a given distance from the market, while the retailer's carries its market with it, sites differing from each other in the size and quality of this market. Moreover, the individual farmer is in the position of a seller in a perfectly competitive market, faced by a demand curve which is, from his point of view, perfectly elastic. The urban retailer is in the position of a monopolist, faced with a sloping demand curve.[12] The several farmers sell in the same market, the urban store has—to some extent— its own market.[13] Chamberlin's conclusion is that the rent paid by retailing activities is monopoly rent, in contrast to that arising in the perfect competition of the agricultural market. This is a thought-provoking distinction, but not fatal to the extension of rent theory from agricultural to urban land uses.

Isard, who has translated agricultural theory into terms of substitution analysis,[14] suggests that ". . . the urban land use problem can be presented in terms of substitution analysis and as an integral part of general location theory, much as agricultural location theory has been. In essence the businessman substitutes among various outlays . . . he incurs additional rent outlays to acquire additional revenue potentials . . . Thus, although the typical businessman may not attack his problem in such a comprehensive fashion, tracing out in a substitution framework what his reactions would be allows us to arrive at optimal patterns of land use."[15]

The analysis below will employ an orthodox or classical substitution analysis to find the equilibrium location of the urban firm.

---

12. This point is not very clear, for agricultural theory finds its equilibrium at the industry level, and it is the demand for the product as a whole that determines rents. This demand is sloped for the industry, if not for the individual farmer.

13. See Chamberlin, *The Theory of Monopolistic Competition*, appendix D, "Urban Rent as Monopoly Income," for these arguments.

14. Essentially of land rent for transport costs. The bid rent function $p_c(t) = N[P_c - C - k_c(t)]$ traces a path where the substitution between increasing transport costs and reduced land costs is such that the entrepreneur is indifferent among locations. "As the enterprise moves away from the market, it substitutes transport outlays for rent outlays, *ceteris paribus*," Isard, *Location and Space-Economy*, p. 196.

15. *Ibid.*, p. 205. It is not clear, however, what is meant by "optimal." Presumably this refers to Haig's "highest and best use," or else to the best location from the point of view of profits for the firm.

However, this analysis of the equilibrium of the firm will suffer from the same shortcomings as the analysis of individual residential equilibrium in the previous chapter. Therefore, in the last pages of this chapter we shall reformulate the equilibrium of the firm in accordance to the principles derived from our analysis of agricultural theory.

A word of explanation is needed, however, before going on with the analysis. What follows is intended to apply to urban firms in general. But, because the language sometimes becomes quite awkward when one tries to describe the behavior of firms in general, the firm will occasionally be viewed as a retail or wholesale concern. The analysis, however, will refer to urban firms in general, including retail and wholesale, office, financial, and manufacturing firms.

General Considerations

In considering the rent of an urban site, Isard cites the following determining factors: "(1) effective distance from the core; (2) accessibility of the site to potential customers; (3) number of competitors, their locations, and the intensity with which they vie for sales; and (4) proximity of land devoted to an individual use or set of uses which are complementary in terms of both attracting potential customers and cutting costs, whether they be production, service, advertising, or other."[16] Chamberlin adds "the prices that can be charged and the type of business which can best be conducted on the location." We shall consider the first of Isard's factors, the distance from the core. In our completely centralized city this implies the second factor; accessibility of the site to potential customers will decrease with distance from the center. The other factors, which relate to the interdependence of business locations, are too complex for analysis here.[17] The tendency of certain businesses to spread or gather may best be understood by Lösch's theory[18] in the former case and by the less clearly formulated theory of linkages in the latter.

16. Isard, *Location and Space-Economy*, p. 200.

17. The consideration of mark-up, to which Isard devotes considerable attention, can probably be explicitly incorporated into the analysis presented here. However, this has not been done at this writing. It is assumed that the firm will have optimized mark-ups, or else that they remain constant.

18. August Lösch, *The Economics of Location* (New Haven: Yale University Press, 1954).

The businessman in this case is very like the resident we considered in chapter 2. He is faced with a given structure of prices[19] for land, according to distance, which is described by the function $P(t)$. He will decide on his location and on the amount of land he wishes to occupy[20] in such a way that he will make the greatest possible profits. These profits may be defined as the remainder after operating costs and land costs have been deducted from the volume of business. This relation may be expressed in the following equation:

$$(3:1) \qquad\qquad G = V - C - R,$$

where G: profits, in dollars;
V: volume of business, in dollars;
C: operating costs, in dollars;
R: land costs, in dollars.

Let us examine the elements of the right-hand side of equation $(3:1)$. The volume of business, V, will depend on the location of the firm, t, and on the size of the site, q, used for selling, display, parking, and inventory. This may be expressed as

$$(3:2) \qquad\qquad V = V(t, q).$$

The operating costs, C, will depend on the location, t, in such matters as distance from warehousing and transportation terminals, and on the size of the site, q, in such matters as maintenance and ease of handling merchandise within the store. Of course, operating costs will also depend on the volume of business, V. Thus operating costs, C, will be a function

$$(3:3) \qquad\qquad C = C(V, t, q).$$

Site rent has been purposely abstracted from these costs to receive

19. We return now to using the word "price" rather than "rent" for the reasons given in the first chapter.

20. The size of the site is seldom if ever considered in the literature, most references being to rent for the site without mention of size. However, it should be clear that market equilibrium cannot be found without consideration of quantities. A notable exception to this neglect is found in Marshall, *Principles of Economics*, book V, chap. XI: "... industries are willing to pay a high value for additional land in order to avoid the inconveniences and expense of crowding their work onto a narrow site" (p. 450), and "If land is cheap he will take much of it; if it is dear he will take less and build high" (p. 448).

separate treatment. The businessman's site rent, R, will be the number of units of land he occupies, q, times the price of land at his location, $P(t)$:

$$(3:4) \qquad\qquad R = P(t)q.$$

The businessman will seek to maximize his profits by adjusting his location and ground space.[21] The marginal analysis of profit maximization could be shown diagrammatically in three dimensions, but it would be extremely difficult to read such a diagram. Consequently, only two-dimensional partial solutions will be shown diagrammatically, and the complete solution will be derived mathematically.

Diagrammatic Solution

First, let us assume that the businessman's location has already been fixed at $t = t_0$. The only variable he can manipulate to maximize profits will be the quantity of land, q. Marginal revenue (changes in V) will eventually decrease as q increases, and will eventually become negative when the store reaches excessive size. (See Figure 13.) Marginal costs consist of changes in operating costs, C, which are shown as decreasing with economies of scale (though, of course, they may increase after the premises reach a certain size) and the marginal cost of land, which remains constant at the price of land at that location, $P(t_0)$. Total marginal costs are the sum of marginal operating costs and the marginal cost of land. The most profitable amount of land will be q_e in Figure 13, where marginal costs equal marginal revenues. The dashed line, indicating marginal profits, is derived by subtracting total marginal costs from marginal revenues. It is positive up to q_e, and negative thereafter. If the businessman had a site smaller than q_e it would pay him to acquire additional land since the marginal costs would be smaller than the marginal revenue. However, he would not expand beyond q_e because mar-

---

21. Implicit in this is the problem of floor-area ratio. For completeness, we should include the firm's consideration of the number of stories in the structure and of the marginal costs of vertical versus horizontal expansion. However, in order to keep the analysis simple this has not been done. It should be noted that Marshall has something to say on this point. He writes of a "margin of building," such that an additional floor will be added "instead of spreading the building over more ground, [when] a saving in the cost of land is effected, which just compensates for the extra expense and inconvenience of the plan" (*ibid.*, p. 448).

ginal costs would be greater than marginal revenues. Thus, the marginal analysis with respect to the size of the site is of the type usually encountered in classical economics.

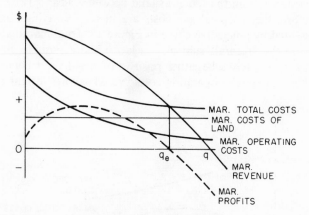

FIGURE 13. Marginal costs and revenue of the firm according to size of site, at a given location

Let us now consider the size of the site as fixed at $q = q_0$, and allow distance t to vary. As the distance from the core of the city increases, sales (revenue) would decrease. This is shown in Figure 14. This means that marginal revenue is negative as in Figure 15. Marginal costs are more complex. There are two components: operating

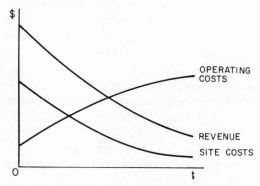

FIGURE 14. Costs and revenue of the firm according to location, holding the size of the site constant

costs and rent. Operating costs will increase with distance from the center (Figure 14), and consequently marginal operating costs will be positive (Figure 15).[22] The other component, rent, will diminish with distance from the center as land becomes cheaper (Figure 14). Therefore, the marginal site costs are in reality savings, and are represented by a negative curve in Figure 15. Total marginal costs, then, are the algebraic sum of a negative and a positive quantity, and may themselves be either positive or negative, depending on whether increases in operating costs exceed savings in rent or not.

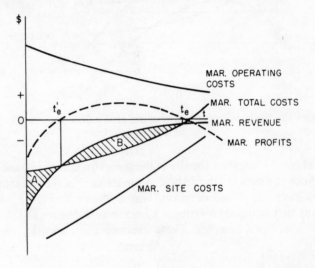

FIGURE 15. Marginal costs and revenue of the firm according to location, holding the size of the site constant

The dashed line representing marginal profits is the result of the algebraic sum of marginal revenues and marginal costs.

The equilibrium location will be at t_e in Figure 15, where marginal revenue equals marginal cost. This is not affected by the meeting of the curves in the negative quadrant. In the situation depicted in the diagram marginal costs are savings and marginal

22. In Figure 15 marginal operating costs have been shown as decreasing with distance because they are probably associated principally with transport costs, which in general increase at a decreasing rate.

revenue is gross income lost with movement away from the center of the city. Maximum profits, and equilibrium, will be achieved at that location (t_e) as long as marginal revenue intersects marginal costs from above. At the earlier intersection, t'_e, marginal revenue intersects marginal costs from below, and consequently further increases in distance would be profitable.

The fact that the marginal revenue curve cuts the marginal costs curve from above at some point is no guarantee, however, that that is an equilibrium point. In Figure 15 there are two shaded areas, *A* and *B*. Area *A* is the total loss involved in moving from the center to t'_e, whereas *B* is the gain in moving from t'_e to t_e. Obviously, then, area *B* must be larger than area *A* for t_e to be the equilibrium location. If area *A* is larger, profits will be maximized at the center where $t = 0$.[23]

Mathematical Solution

While the optimization of location and size of site have just been presented separately, the equilibrium of the firm requires their simultaneous solution. This can best be done through differential equations. A particular advantage of the mathematical approach is its generality. In the diagrammatic solution, above, we considered a case in which the volume of business decreased with increasing distance from the center of the city. However, in the case of a manufacturing concern, location may not affect the volume of business. In the mathematical solution, the first case would have a negative partial derivative of *V* with respect to distance, while in the second case the value of the partial derivative would be zero. Thus, a single solution will be general and embrace all possible cases. The equations representing revenue, costs, and profits for the firm, it will be

23. The other diagrammatic possibilities are covered by this criterion. (1) If the marginal revenue curve is at all points below the marginal costs curve, area *A* is infinite and area *B* is zero. Profits will be maximized at the center. (2) If the marginal revenue curve is over the marginal costs curve at all points before the intersection at t_e, and below beyond that point, area *A* will be zero, area *B* will be finite but greater than zero, and profits will be maximized at t_e. (3) For logical completeness, we should consider the possibility of the marginal revenue curve being above the marginal costs curve at all points to infinity. Then area *A* would be zero, area *B* would be of undefined size, possibly infinite, and a location at an infinite distance from the city would be optimal. A moment's thought will show this to be absurd.

remembered, are:

(3:1)   profits $G = V - C - R$

(3:2)   volume of business $V = V(t, q)$

(3:3)   operating costs $C = C(V, t, q)$

(3:4)   land costs $R = P(t)q.$

Our problem is, given the function $P(t)$, to maximize profits, G. Differentiating equation (3:1), we obtain

$$dG = dV - dC - dR.$$

Since G is being maximized, $dG = 0$, and

(3:5) $0 = dG = dV - dC - dR.$

Differentiating equations (3:2, 3, 4) yields

$$dV = V_t \, dt + V_q \, dq$$
$$dC = C_V \, dV + C_t \, dt + C_q \, dq^{24}$$
$$dR = P(t)dq + q(dP/dt)dt.$$

Substituting these into equation (3:5):

$$0 = dG = V_t \, dt + V_q \, dq - C_V \, dV - C_q \, dq - C_t \, dt - P \, dq - q(dP/dt)dt.$$

Substituting again for dV in the third term of the right-hand side of the equation,

$$0 = dG = V_t \, dt + V_q \, dq - C_V(V_t \, dt + V_q \, dq)$$
$$- C_q \, dq - C_t \, dt - P \, dq - q(dP/dt)dt.$$

This may be rewritten as

(3:6) $0 = dt(V_t - C_V V_t - C_t - q \, dP/dt) + dq(V_q - C_V V_q - C_q - P).$

Holding q constant in equation (3:6), so that $dq = 0$, we have

$$0 = dt(V_t - C_V V_t - C_t - q \, dP/dt),$$

from which, since $dt \neq 0$, dividing through by dt,

(3:7) $0 = V_t - C_V V_t - C_t - q \, dP/dt.$

24. Here C_t and C_q are partials of $C(V, t, q)$, considering V as a third independent variable. The dependence of V on t and q is introduced below.

Conversely, holding t constant so that $dt=0$, equation (3:6) becomes

$$0 = dq(V_q - C_V V_q - C_q - P),$$

and, since $dq \neq 0$, dividing through by dq, we obtain

(3:8) $0 = V_q - C_V V_q - C_q - P.$

The two equations (3:7, 8) enable us to solve for the two unknowns, t and q, since all the variables are expressed parametrically in terms of these two. The values of G, V, C, and R can be calculated from equations (3:1, 2, 3, 4) by putting in the appropriate values of t and q. Of course, the necessary steps must be taken, where there are multiple solutions, to find the *maximum maximorum*. The absolute value of G at the center ($t=0$) should be tested, with equation (3:8) holding, for dP/dt is discontinuous there.

Interpretation of the Mathematical Solution

Equations (3:7, 8) are of the usual form, stating that at equilibrium, profits having been maximized, marginal cost must equal marginal revenue. In this sense, they are restatements of Figures 13 and 15. Verbally, we may interpret the terms of these equations as follows:

Location equation: (3:7) $0 = V_t - C_V V_t - C_t - q\, dP/dt$.

  V_t: marginal revenue lost from moving an additional distance dt away from the center;

  $C_V V_t$: marginal operating cost (presumably negative) arising from the change in volume of business V_t (indirect effect of movement on operating costs);

  C_t: marginal increases in operating costs arising directly from movement dt;

  $q\, dP/dt$: decrease in rent payments arising from the change in the price of land with movement dt;

Size of site equation: (3:8) $0 = V_q - C_V V_q - C_q - P$.

  V_q: marginal change in the volume of sales arising from the increase in area dq;

  $C_V V_q$: change in operating costs arising from the change in the volume of sales arising from the increase in area (indirect effect of the change in area on operating costs);

C_q: marginal change in operating costs arising directly
     from the increase in area, dq;
P: cost of the marginal unit of area.

D. Derivation of the Bid Price Curves of the Urban Firm

In section B of this chapter it was noted that in the agricultural
models a set of bid rent functions was derived for each farmer, such
that he was indifferent as to his location along any one of these
functions. We shall now establish a family of such curves for the
urban firm. They will be called, however, bid price rather than bid
rent functions for the reasons adduced in the first chapter. Though
the analysis must be pursued much further before arriving at the
market equilibrium solution, this chapter will conclude with a
demonstration of how these curves may be used to find the equilibrium location of the firm.

We wish to derive a bid price function for the urban firm, such
that the firm would be indifferent among locations at these prices.
This would occur if all locations yielded the firm the same profits.
It is clear that such a bid price function bears no necessary relation
to actual prices. It is a hypothetical price-of-land-with-distance
function, and might be termed an iso-profit curve. In short, it
merely says: if price of land varied thus with location, the firm
would make the same profits at any location, and consequently it
would be indifferent among locations. (In chapter 4 we shall explore
the similarities and differences between indifference curves and bid
rent functions.)

We shall denote this function as

$$p_f(t) \llbracket G_0$$

which may be read as the price (p) bid by a firm (f) at each location
t, such that, when the quantity of land is optimized, the firm can
achieve a constant level of profits G_0, and no more. Since the level
of profits is constant, the firm will be indifferent as to its location.
Where the referees (f, G_0) are clear, we shall abbreviate this
notation to

$$p(t).$$

In the future, the capital letter P will refer to an actual price, the lower case p to a bid price. We shall now show how such a bid price curve may be derived.

The bid price function describes prices that the firm would be willing to pay in order to make exactly G_0 profits. The quantity of land at each location will be optimized to make the maximum profits. Therefore, the equation for the optimization of land (3:8) will hold at every location. In our new notation this now reads

$$0 = V_q - C_V V_q - C_q - p_f(t) [G_0,$$

or, in the abbreviated notation,

(3:9) $$0 = V_q - C_V V_q - C_q - p(t).$$

The original set of equations (3:1, 2, 3, 4), must, of course, continue to hold. They will now be written:

(3:10) $$G_0 = V - C - R$$

(3:11) $$V = V(t, q)$$

(3:12) $$C = C(V, t, q)$$

(3:13) $$R = p(t)q.$$

We have, then, five equations (3:9, 10, 11, 12, 13), and six variables: $p_f(t) [G_0, q, t, V, C, R$. We may therefore designate one of these variables as a parameter, in terms of which to express the others. Therefore, the expression $p(t)$, which thus far has been a notational device to designate p, now becomes a function in which bid price, p, is uniquely defined by the single variable, t. This is the bid price function.

There are a number of corollaries to be proved concerning the properties of this function:

(1) *The bid price function is single-valued.* This means that, for any given level of profits, G_0, there is one and only one value of p possible at any given t. (See appendix G, note 1 for the formal proof.)

(2) *Two bid price curves, corresponding to different levels of profits for the same firm, will not cross.* (See appendix G, note 2 for the formal proof.) These two corollaries enable us to use an alternative notation for bid price curves. Since they are

single-valued and do not cross, any such curve can be identified by any point on it. It is possible to use the notation

$$p_f(t) \llbracket t_0, p_0,$$

where t_0, p_0 is any point on the curve (that is, $p_0 = p_f(t_0) \llbracket t_0, p_0)$, rather than using the level of profits as the referee, as in the notation $p_f(t) \llbracket G_0$. This new notation will be preferred since it will permit direct comparison of bid prices among urban firms, residences, and agriculture.

(3) *The lower bid price curves represent higher levels of profits, and consequently are preferable from the point of view of the firm.* This is obvious since profits are a residual after operating costs and land costs are paid, so that the lower the price of land, the higher the residual profits. This implies that curves above the curve for zero profits ($G = 0$), correspond to operation at a loss, and may be disregarded. The firm would not choose to enter the market at a loss, and would not make such bids.

(4) *Bid price functions in general will slope downward.* This may be expected from common sense: since, as a rule, revenue decreases and operating costs increase with distance, bid prices must decrease for the level of profits to remain constant. This slope (whether or not negative) may be stated precisely. (See appendix G, note 3 for the derivation).

$$(3:14) \qquad dp/dt = (V_t - C_V V_t - C_t)/q.$$

The change in bid price is equal to the change in the volume of business minus the change in operating costs, divided through by the quantity of land so as to obtain a per-unit-of-land figure. Since, as a rule, (1) the volume of business will decrease with increasing distance, so that V_t is negative, (2) operating costs will rise, so that change will be positive, but preceded by a minus sign,[25] and (3) the quantity of land must be positive, the slope of the bid price curve must be negative.

---

25. The term $C_V V_t$, representing the indirect decrease in operating costs arising from the decrease in the volume of sales, will be negative. As it is preceded by a minus sign, its effect will be positive. However, the marginal costs per marginal change in volume of business must be less than unity at any equilibrium position, so that $(V_t - C_V V_t) < 0$.

The slope will be such that the savings in land costs are just equal to the business lost plus the increase in operating costs.

In short, then, a family of bid price curves for a firm is very like an indifference map: the curves are single-valued, do not cross, and slope downward to the right. However, though both indicate a preference mapping, in the case of bid price curves, preference is downward rather than upward.[26] Equally important is the comparison with the agricultural bid rent curve. Both families of curves are such that the user is indifferent as to his location along any one of these functions. Both, as will be shown in chapter 5, can be used in the same way to find the highest bidder, urban firm, or farmer, for a location. They differ in that each bid rent function in the agricultural family corresponds to a different market price for the agricultural produce, while profits to the farmer are held constant throughout at "normal profits." On the other hand, in the bid price mapping of the urban firm, each curve corresponds to a different level of profits, while prices (p_z) are assumed either held constant or adjusted by the firm as in the usual monopoly problem.

Another difference between the bid price curves of the urban firm and the bid rent curves of the agricultural sector is that, in the latter, the individual farmer has no preference as to higher and lower curves, since his profits are everywhere "normal." The level of the curves is determined by a combination of derived demand for the product and the entry and exit into the market of producers. As will be seen below, in the urban case the level of the curve is determined by comparing the preferences of the firm with the opportunities available to it.

Yet another significant difference is that there is no highest agricultural bid rent curve or indifference curve. The price of a commodity and the level of satisfaction of an individual have no logically necessary upper limit. The highest bid price function of an urban firm, on the other hand, will be that for which its profits are zero. Higher curves are conceptually possible, but they would mean that the firm would operate at a loss. Accordingly, the firm would not make these bids for land.

---

26. The more complex question of what is measured on the axes in either type of analysis is examined in chapter 4, where a bid price curve mapping for a resident will be derived from his indifference map.

E. Equilibrium of the Urban Firm through Bid Price Curves

In Figure 16 a map of bid price curves for a firm is shown. According to our notation, curves BPC_1, BPC_2, and BPC_3 are, respectively, $p_f(t)[\![t_i, p_i,\ p_f(t)[\![t_i, p_i',$ and $p_f(t)[\![t_i, p_i''.$ From the point of view of the firm, BPC_1 is preferable to BPC_2, which in turn is preferable to BPC_3. The firm is faced with an existing structure of land prices $P(t)$ such as that in Figure 17. Figure 16 represents a mapping of

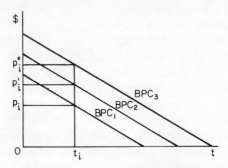

FIGURE 16. Diagrammatic mapping of bid price curves

the firm's preferences, while Figure 17 is a mapping of the opportunities available to it; preferences and opportunities are shown in the same diagram in Figure 18. The firm will locate at the point at which the price structure touches the lowest of the bid price curves with which it comes in contact.[27] At this point, t_e in Figure 18, the profits of the firm are maximized.[28]

The diagram does not tell us what the optimal quantity of land at this point will be, but this is not important. The bid price curve was defined in such a way that it took into account the optimization of the quantity of land for that price and location. Once the location and the price are known, finding the quantity of land is a simple problem corresponding to Figure 13. The quantity may be computed from equations (3:1, 2, 3, 4). Alternatively, just as we found

27. If the highest bid price curve, for which profits are zero, is at all points below the price structure, the firm can nowhere operate except at a loss and will not enter the market.

28. A price structure more concave from the origin than the bid price curves would yield end point locations.

the parametric form $p_f(t)[\![G_0$ in section D, we can at the same time find the parametric form for optimal land quantities as a function of distance for that level of profits.

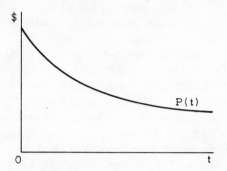

FIGURE 17. Diagrammatic price structure

At the point where $P(t)$ comes in contact with BPC_2 in Figure 18, the two curves are tangent. If they were not, they would intersect, and there would exist some bid price curve below BPC_2 which would be in contact with $P(t)$ and yield a higher level of profits. In other words, at that point the slopes of the two curves are equal:

$$\frac{d}{dt}pf(t_c)[\![t_c, p_c = \frac{dP(t_c)}{dt}.$$

To the left of t_c, $P(t)$ is steeper than the bid price curve. Since the

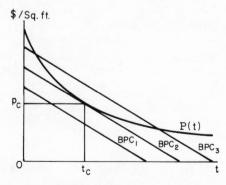

FIGURE 18. Diagrammatic bid prices and price structure: equilibrium of the firm

slope of the bid price curve is the change in the price of land necessary to offset the loss in sales and the increased operating costs, where $P(t)$ is steeper the savings in land costs exceed the loss of revenue and the increased operating costs of outward movement, and the firm would increase its profits by moving farther out. To the right of t_c, on the other hand, the bid price curve is steeper than the actual price structure, meaning that the savings on land are not sufficient to offset lost sales and increased operating costs. The firm would move to the left and come to equilibrium at t_c.[29]

Nothing new has been added to the equilibrium of the firm in this analysis. The equilibrium position was found, without using bid price curves, in section B of this chapter. In the last two sections the same assumptions have been marshaled in another way to arrive at the same conclusions. The point of this exercise has been to gain a view of the equilibrium of the firm such that it may be used as a starting point for arriving at the market equilibrium. In the next chapter residential consumer bid price curves will be derived and used to find individual equilibrium. After that, in chapter 5, we shall arrive at a market solution.

---

29. Where the lowest bid price curve and the price structure come in contact at the center of the city, the curves need not be tangent. In fact, since there is no left-hand derivative at that point, they cannot be tangent in the full sense. However, to the right the bid price curve must be steeper than the price structure. The reader can visualize this condition by viewing Figure 18 as having the origin at t_c.

4

Residential Bid Price Curves

A. INTRODUCTION

In this chapter we shall derive bid price curves for the individual resident and use them to find individual equilibrium. The mathematical derivation is quite brief, but to make the concept clearer, a section will be devoted to the diagrammatic derivation of bid price curves from the indifference mapping.

A bid price curve of a resident is the set of prices for land the individual could pay at various distances while deriving a constant level of satisfaction; that is to say, if price of land were to vary with distance in the manner described by the bid price curve, the individual would be indifferent among locations. Three points must be emphasized. The first is that a bid price curve refers to a given individual: other individuals may have differently shaped bid price curves in the same way the bid rent functions of different crops differ. The second is that a bid price curve refers to a given level of satisfaction. Since there is an infinite number of levels of satisfaction for an individual, there will be for each individual a family of bid price curves corresponding to different levels of satisfaction. The third point that requires emphasis is that a bid price bears no necessary relation to the actual price that is charged for the use of land at that location. A bid price is hypothetical, merely saying that, if the price of land were such, the individual would be satisfied to a given degree.

B. DIAGRAMMATIC DERIVATION OF BID PRICE

Let us consider the case of an individual, i, who, for whatever reason, must locate at t_0. Given (1) a price of land p_0,[1] (2) his income, y_i, (3) his costs of commuting, $k(t_0)$, and (4) the price, p_z, of

1. As in the case of the urban firm, the hypothetical bid prices will be denoted by the lower case p, while the capital P will be used for the price of an actual transaction.

the composite good z, his choice will be determined in the traditional manner of consumer equilibrium (see chapter 2). His indifference curves between q and z will be shaped in the ordinary fashion, convex toward the origin, as curve $I_{i,0}$ in Figure 19.[2] His locus of opportunities, from equation (2:1) in chapter 2, is described by

$$y_i - k(t_0) = p_z z + p_0 q,$$

which may be rewritten as

$$q = [y_i - k(t_0)]/p_0 - (p_z/p_0)z.$$

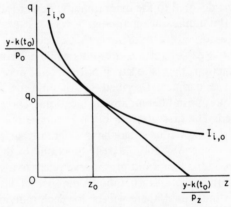

FIGURE 19. Locus of opportunities and equilibrium indifference curve between q and z, at a given t_0

This is an ordinary budget line: a straight line with the slope $-p_z/p_0$, and intercepts $[y_i - k(t_0)]/p_0$ on the q-axis and $[y_i - k(t_0)]/p_z$ on the z-axis.[3]

Equilibrium will be at the point of tangency between the locus of opportunities and the highest of the indifference curves with which it comes in contact. The combination of q and z at this point is the most satisfying to him from the choices he has available. This is

2. See chapter 2, Figure 7, and trace $QRST$ on the B-plane in Figure 10 for the relation to the whole indifference surface.

3. See in chapter 2, Figure 2 and line VS in Figure 5 for the relation to the whole locus of opportunities surface.

point q_0, z_0 in Figure 19. When distance is given, then the problem is but a part of the one considered in section B of chapter 2.

Now we ask the question: what price of land, p_m, at location t_m, would allow the individual to enjoy as much satisfaction? By definition, this will be the price that enables the individual to remain on the indifference surface of which $I_{i,0}$ is the trace at t_0 in Figure 19. Curve $I_{i,m}$ in Figure 20 is the trace of that indifference surface at t_m, and thus represents the same level of satisfaction.

The individual will have a variety of choices as to how to spend his money between q and z, no matter what price p_m turns out to be.

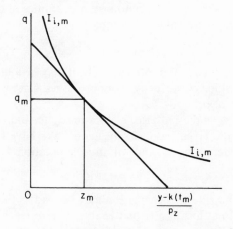

FIGURE 20. Derived locus of opportunities and equilibrium indifference curve between q and z, at a given t_m

These choices will be represented by a straight line locus of opportunity, since from equation (2:1) we obtain the linear relation

$$y_i - k(t_m) = p_z z + p_m q.$$

Two questions now arise: (1) is there more than one price p_m which satisfies the definition?, and (2) how can it (they) be found?

Let us answer the second question first. We have just observed that the locus of opportunities, from equation (2:1), will be a straight line. The intercept on the z-axis is independent of the value of p_m, and may be calculated from equation (2:1) to be $[y_i - k(t_m)]/p_z$.

Since the individual will be maximizing his satisfaction by adjusting his purchases of q and z and since, by definition, he will be able to achieve the satisfaction represented by indifference curve $I_{i,m}$, the derived locus of opportunities must be tangent to the indifference curve. Accordingly, all that is necessary is to draw all straight lines passing through $q=0$, $z=[y_i-k(t_m)]/p_z$ which are tangent to $I_{i,m}$. How many of these lines will there be?: from examination of Figure 20, it is clear that only one line will satisfy these conditions. (See appendix H, note 1 for the formal proof.)

Once the locus of opportunities line has been derived, the price of land p_m may be easily found. The co-ordinates of the point of tangency, q_m and z_m, are the equilibrium quantities of these goods. By substituting these values into equation (2:1)

$$y_i = p_z z_m + p_m q_m + k(t_m),$$

the price p_m may be found. Alternatively, it may be found by dividing p_z by the slope of the locus of opportunities, since we know this slope to be $-p_z/p_m$.

This price p_m is the bid price at location t_m for individual i with reference to the given level of satisfaction. We have denoted this level of satisfaction by u_0, and will use the notation

$$p_m = p_i(t_m)[\![u_0.$$

The right-hand side of the equation may be read as the price p bid by individual i at location t_m that enables him to reach satisfaction u_0. However, since we arrived at this bid price by comparison with price at another location (p_0 at t_0), as well as by fixing the level of satisfaction, we will prefer the notation

$$p_m = p_i(t_m)[\![t_0, p_0.$$

The advantage of using such a referee rather than a level of satisfaction is that it uses measurable quantities rather than the subjective and arbitrarily numbered indifference level.

Having obtained a bid price at t_m, the next task is to find it for all values of t. This will give us a function $p_i(t)[\![t_0, p_0$, where bid price for every value of t is given in terms of the same referee. Such a function can be inferred from the derived locus of opportunities surface in Figure 21, though the process requires some explanation. The figure shows the full indifference surface, u_0, of which $I_{i,0}$ and

$I_{i,m}$ are sections. The diagrams of Figures 19 and 20 reappear here at t_0 and t_m. At every other value of t, a locus of opportunities curve has been erected in precisely the manner in which it was done at t_m. These curves, when considered together, form a locus of opportunities surface (*LO* in Figure 21) such that, given the amount that

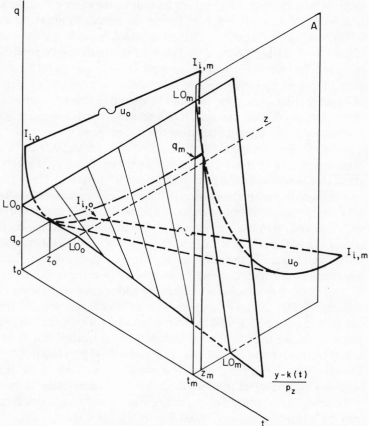

FIGURE 21. An indifference surface, u_0, and its derived locus of opportunities

can be spent at each location, $y_i - k(t)$, and the price p_z, the consumer can at all locations reach the indifference surface u_0 and no higher. That is to say, the derived locus of opportunities fulfills the budget requirement and is tangent to u_0 at every t. At every location the slope of the *LO*-surface in the q–z plane will be the ratio of the prices of q and z: $-p_z/p_i(t)$.[4] Consequently, dividing the constant p_z by this ratio will yield the bid price at any location.

This derived locus of opportunities is based on bid prices, $p(t)$, and has been constructed to represent the hypothetical conditions under which the individual would be indifferent among locations. It should not be confused with the actual locus of opportunities facing him, as in Figure 5 in chapter 2, which is based on the real structure of market prices, $P(t)$. Whereas the individual's equilibrium indifference curve will be tangent at only one point to his actual locus of opportunities, we may construct one derived locus of opportunities surface for each of the infinite indifference surfaces of the individual, such that each indifference surface is tangent to its derived locus of opportunities over the full range of t.

Examination of Figure 21 reveals that the derived *LO*-surface becomes steeper in the q–z plane as t increases. Since p_z is a constant, this means that bid price decreases with distance. There are two geometric reasons for this: (1) the indifference surface moves away from the t-axis both vertically and horizontally (see Figures 6, 7, 8, 9, and 10 in chapter 2); and (2) increasing commuting costs reduce the z-intercept of the *LO*-surface, $[y_i - k(t)]/p_z$, as t increases.

The significance of the latter point, that commuting costs reduce bid price as distance increases, can be readily understood. Commuting costs, $k(t)$, increase with distance and reduce the amount of money, $y_i - k(t)$, the individual has at his disposal to spend on the goods he cares about (q and z). To compensate for this, the price of q must drop, so that, land being cheaper, the individual can maintain the same level of satisfaction with his reduced effective income. In other words, the price of q must drop just sufficiently for the resulting income-effect to offset the increase in commuting costs.

The effect of the other factor, the shape of the indifference surface, may be harder to visualize from Figure 21. Its common sense is clear, however: the added nuisance of commuting requires the compensation of cheaper land for the consumer to maintain the same level of satisfaction. This effect may be illustrated very clearly in a simplified example.

4. When the referee of the bid price curve is clear, it will be omitted. Thus, $p_i(t)$ here stands for $p_i(t)[\![t_0, p_0$.

Let us take a very simple case in which the individual has a fixed amount of money, R, to spend on land. There are no commuting costs, so that regardless of location,

$$R = p_i(t)q.$$

Because R is a constant, the individual's demand curve for land at any location will be a rectangular hyperbola such as D_i in Figure 22. There being no commuting costs, this curve will be the same regardless of location, so that we may represent the individual's demand

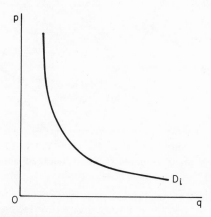

FIGURE 22. Individual's demand for land when the amount to be spent is constant

for land at every location by surface D_i in Figure 23. The tastes of the individual are represented by the indifference curve I_0 in Figure 24. It will be remembered that indifference curves between land and distance are positively inclined.

We are trying to find the bid price curve, $p_i(t)$, that will enable the individual to remain at the level of satisfaction represented by curve I_0 while satisfying the budget condition $R = p_i(t)q$. The indifference curve states the amount of land the individual requires at every location to maintain this level of satisfaction. The demand surface D_i, which is the graphic representation of the budget condition, tells us at what price the individual would purchase that amount of land.

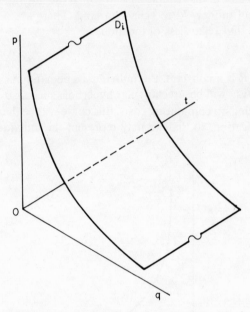

FIGURE 23. Individual's demand surface when the amount to be spent for land is constant

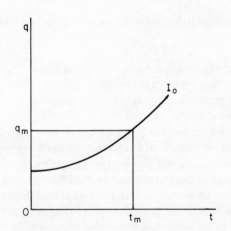

FIGURE 24. Indifference curve of land and distance

Graphically, the matter is fairly simple. On Figure 25 is drawn the demand surface D_i, and, on the t–q plane, the indifference curve I_0. By projecting the indifference curve onto the surface D_i, we obtain the trace represented by the dotted line ss. The three-dimensional curve ss consists of the combinations of q, t, and p which enable the

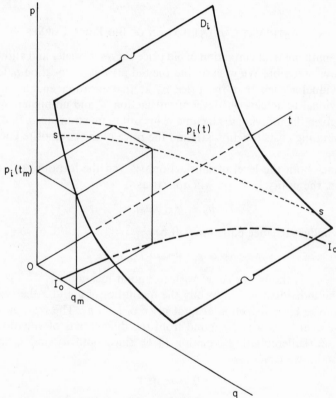

FIGURE 25. Diagrammatic derivation of a bid price curve when the amount to be spent for land is constant

individual to maintain his level of satisfaction and to satisfy his budget balance. To abstract the variation of price with distance under these conditions, the curve ss is projected onto the p–t plane. This projection is a function of p in terms of t, and this function is precisely bid price, $p_i(t)$. It is a hypothetical price structure such that all locations are equally preferable from the point of view of individual i. It will be noted that the positive slope of the indifference curve, when reflected off the downward sloping demand surface, results in a negatively sloped bid price curve. Thus, even in the absence of commuting costs, bid price curves are negatively sloped.

C. Mathematical Derivation of Bid Price Curves

The mathematical derivation of bid price curves is briefer and allows greater precision. We wish to find the bid price p_0 at location t_0 for individual i such that the price p_0 at that location enables the individual to achieve the level of satisfaction u_0 and no higher. We are given the individual's income y, his utility function $u(z, q, t)$, the commuting costs function $k(t)$ and the price of the composite good p_z.

Since both the level of satisfaction, u_0, and the location, t_0, are given, the utility function will appear as

$$(4:1) \qquad u_0 = u(z, q, t_0).$$

The budget balance equation will be

$$(4:2) \qquad y = p_z z + p_0 q + k(t_0),$$

where p_0 is the bid price we wish to find at location t_0.

The individual is free to buy the quantities of q and z that will maximize his satisfaction at t_0 at price of land p_0. The relation of these quantities may be found from the differentials of equations (4:1, 2). Differentiating equation (4:1), since both u_0 and t_0 are constant, we have

$$(4:3) \qquad du_0 = 0 = u_z \, dz + u_q \, dq.$$

When we differentiate equation (4:2), since y, p_0, and t_0 are constant,

$$(4:4) \qquad dy = 0 = p_z \, dz + p_0 \, dq.$$

From equations (4:3, 4), we obtain

$$(4:5) \qquad u_q/u_z = p_0/p_z.$$

We now have three equations (4:1, 2, 5) with which we can find our three unknowns (z, q, p_0). The price p_0 at t_0 will be the price bid by individual i at that location, using the level of satisfaction u_0 as a referee:

$$p_0 = p_i(t_0)[\![u_0.$$

We now wish to find bid price as a function of distance. This may be derived from equations (4:1, 2, 5). Instead of regarding distance as a given t_0, we now regard it as a variable, t. Bid price at any location will be denoted by $p_i(t)$. Equations (4:1, 2, 5) can be rewritten

$$(4:6) \qquad u_0 = u(z, q, t),$$

$$(4:7) \qquad y = p_z z + p_i(t) q + k(t), \quad \text{and}$$

$$(4:8) \qquad u_q/u_z = p_i(t)/p_z.$$

We now have three simultaneous equations (4:6, 7, 8), and four variables $(z, q, p_i(t), t)$. We may regard any one of these variables as a parameter in terms of which the other three variables may be expressed. We choose t as a parameter, and the parametric equation $p_i(t)[\![t_0, p_0$ is the bid price function.

Some corollaries must be proven concerning residential bid price curves:

(1) *The bid price curve is single-valued.* That is to say, at any location, there will be only one bid price that satisfies the conditions. (See appendix H, note 2 for the formal proof.)

(2) *Lower bid price curves imply greater satisfaction.*[5] This is common sense: the lower curves signify lower land prices. (See appendix H, note 2 for the formal proof.)

(3) *Bid price curves for the same individual do not cross.* (See appendix H, note 3 for the formal proof.) Since the curves are single-valued and do not cross, any point p_0, t_0 on the curve

---

5. However, in contrast with the case of the urban firm, there is no logically necessary highest bid price curve for the family of residential bid price curves. Higher and higher curves will yield less and less satisfaction. But the individual must have a place to live, and he must content himself, if necessary, with more and more crowded living conditions.

identifies the curve. We may therefore use the alternative notation

$$p_i(t)[\![t_0, p_0 = p_i(t)[\![u_0$$

where $p_0 = p_i(t_0)[\![u_0.$

Though the form of the bid price curve cannot be stated explicitly without knowing the form of the utility function, the slope of the bid price curve can be stated with some precision. The bid price curve was defined in equations (4:6, 7, 8) above. Equations (4:6, 7) are necessary to find the slope of the curve:

$$(4:6) \qquad\qquad u_0 = u(z, q, t)$$

$$(4:7) \qquad\qquad y = p_z z + p_i(t)q + k(t).$$

When we differentiate, we obtain:

$$du_0 = 0 = u_z\, dz + u_q\, dq + u_t\, dt$$

$$dy = 0 = p_z\, dz + p_i(t)dq + q[dp_i(t)/dt]dt + [dk/dt]dt.$$

Holding q constant so that $dq = 0$, these two equations may be rewritten:

$$-dz/dt = u_t/u_z$$

$$-dz/dt = [q\, dp_i(t)/dt + dk/dt]/p_z.$$

Combining these two:

$$(4:9) \qquad\qquad u_t/u_z = [q\, dp_i(t)/dt + dk/dt]/p_z.$$

The slope of the bid price curve, dp_i/dt,[6] can be shown to be negative in equation (4:9). Distance has a marginal disutility, so that u_t is negative. Both the price and the marginal utility of z are positive, so that both sides of the equation must be negative. But, on the right-hand side, both the quantity of land q and the marginal cost of commuting dk/dt are positive. Consequently dp_i/dt must be negative, and bid price must decrease with distance from the center of the city.

---

6. The notation dp_i/dt is used for brevity instead of $dp_i(t)/dt$, or the fuller
$$\frac{d}{dt}p_i(t)[\![t_0, p_0.$$

To see precisely what causes bid price to drop let us rewrite equation (4:9) as

(4:10)
$$\frac{dp_i}{dt} = \frac{p_z}{q}\frac{u_t}{u_z} - \frac{1}{q}\frac{dk}{dt}.$$

Both elements of the right-hand side of the equation are negative, so that both contribute to the negative character of the slope of the bid price curve. The first term is negative because of the disutility of distance, while the second represents commuting costs. This is the same conclusion we had reached diagrammatically, namely that both tastes and the costs of commuting make for a diminution of price with distance. Even were there no commuting costs ($dk/dt = 0$), the disutility of distance ($u_t < 0$) would make for a negatively sloped bid price curve.

Equation (4:9) is a marginal rate of substitution equation. The left-hand side, the ratio of the marginal utilities, is the marginal rate of substitution by definition. The right-hand side is the ratio of the marginal costs. Its denominator is the price or marginal cost of z. Its numerator is the marginal cost of movement away from the center of the city. Because outward movement produces disutility, this marginal cost must in effect be a saving in order that the bid price curve maintain a given level of satisfaction. This saving must occur in land costs because commuting costs are increasing. The marginal cost of movement is equal to the quantity of land times the change in the price of land plus the increase in the costs of commuting. Bid price, then, has been defined so that the income effect of cheaper land will counteract the depressing effect of commuting costs on income, and will permit the consumer to maintain a given level of satisfaction by substituting land and the composite good for accessibility as distance from the center increases.

D. INDIVIDUAL EQUILIBRIUM THROUGH BID PRICE CURVES

The concept of bid price is useful in that it permits a solution of individual equilibrium which combines the indifference curve approach with an explicit consideration of land prices. A bid price curve is a set of combinations of land prices and distances among which the individual is indifferent. This differs from an indifference curve which describes combinations of goods among which the individual is indifferent, without consideration of prices. By combining the indifference mapping with the budget balance restriction, we have obtained this hybrid, in which we describe indifference conditions between one good (accessibility, or, rather, the negative good distance) and the price of another good (land). The relation among the quantities of the other good, their prices, and the individual's income are implicit in this curve. What has been done is to take a problem in the five dimensions of utility, land, distance, the composite good, and money, and to present it in summary form in two of these dimensions: distance and the cost of land. (In three dimensions, if we regard the ordering of the family of bid price curves as a projection from an implicit dimension of utility.)

Individual equilibrium may be found in a way parallel to the superimposing of the budget line on the indifference curve mapping in the usual consumer equilibrium problem. The bid price curves represent given levels of indifference, differing from indifference curves in that the lower rather than the higher curves are preferable. The structure of actual prices confronting the individual is a locus of opportunities, equivalent to the budget line in the usual problem: both are mappings of the choices open to the individual. The individual will choose that point of his locus opportunities at which his utility is maximized. In this case, the point will be that at which the price structure touches the lowest of the bid price curves with which it comes in contact. The procedure is identical to that used in chapter 3 to determine the equilibrium of the urban firm. (If an illustration is desired to follow the argument, refer to Figure 18 in chapter 3.) It is not necessary to know whether a family of bid price curves is that of a resident or an urban firm to join them to the price structure and determine the point of equilibrium. In either case, it will be that at which the price structure touches the lowest of the bid price curves with which it comes in contact.

In chapter 3, it was proved that at the point of equilibrium the price structure and the bid price curve must be tangent.[7] This is, of course, true for the residential case as well, but it is illuminating to examine the mathematical expression of this situation. It will be remembered from chapter 2 that, at equilibrium, the individual's marginal rate of substitution between distance from the center of the

7. If they were not tangent, they would cross, and if they crossed, the price structure would come in contact with some lower bid price curve.

city and the composite good is equal to the ratio of their marginal costs:

(2:15) $u_t/u_z = (q\,dP/dt + dk/dt)/p_z$ (at equilibrium).

In this chapter, it has been shown that the slope of the bid price curve is defined by the equation:

(4:9) $u_t/u_z = (q\,dp_i/dt + dk/dt)/p_z$ (at all points).

Comparing these two equations reveals that at equilibrium $dP/dt = dp_i/dt$; that is, the curves are tangent.

To the right and to the left of the point of equilibrium the two curves will diverge. This is no mere graphic necessity: it has a clear economic meaning. To the left, the price structure is steeper than the bid price curve; that is, $dP/dt < dp_i/dt$, and consequently $u_t/u_z > (q\,dP/dt + dk/dt)/p_z$.[8] That is to say, nearer the center of the city, the marginal rate of substitution exceeds the ratio of the marginal costs, and the individual can increase his satisfaction by further movement outward, toward cheaper land. Conversely, farther out from the point of equilibrium, the bid price curve is steeper than the actual price structure; that is, $dP/dt > dp_i/dt$, and consequently $u_t/u_z < (q\,dP/dt + dk/dt)/p_z$. That is to say, the marginal rate of substitution is smaller than the ratio of the marginal costs, and the individual can increase his satisfaction by moving toward the center of the city and reducing the expense and bother of commuting.

E. Bid Price Curves of the Individual Resident and the Urban Firm and Bid Rent Curves of Agriculture: Similarities and Differences

In this chapter and in chapter 3 considerable effort has been devoted to the derivation of bid price curves for the urban firm and resident that would share the properties of the agricultural bid rent curves. This has been done to evolve a method of solution for a land market that embraces the three types of land uses. The relevant properties of these curves are summarized in Table 1.

In column (1) are listed the notations by which each type of bid price or rent may be specified. An agricultural bid rent may be

---

8. In considering the direction of the inequalities it should be remembered that we are dealing with negative values.

TABLE 1. Comparison of notation, importance of variables, and market mechanism of adjustment among agriculture, urban firms, and residences

Land use	Notation		Variables among curves			Mechanism of adjustment		
	Special notation (1)	Common notation (2)	Price of commodity (3)	Profits (4)	Utility (5)	Entry-exit (6)	Preference among curves (7)	Preference along a curve (8)
Agriculture	$p_{ag}(t)\|P_c$	$p_{ag}(t)\|t_0, p_0$	variable	constant	not applicable	unlimited	none	none
Urban firm	$p_f(t)\|G_0$	$p_f(t)\|t_0, p_0$	constant	variable	not applicable	limited	lower curves	none
Residential	$p_f(t)\|u_0$	$p_f(t)\|t_0, p_0$	not applicable	not applicable	variable	none	lower curves	none

defined by the price of the commodity at the market, P_c. A given bid price curve may be specified by the level of profits, G_0, for the urban firm, and by the level of satisfaction, u_0, for the urban resident. However, in all three cases the curves are single-valued and do not cross, so that a particular curve may be denoted in each case by using as a referee any point on the curve (t_0, p_0), as in column (2). Columns (3), (4), and (5) show what varies and what remains constant from curve to curve within the family of curves for each land use. It will be noted that in each case the variable is the referee in the notation of column (1). By using the common referee in the notation of column (2) these variables are made comparable for our purposes.

Columns (6), (7), and (8) refer to the mechanism by which equilibrium of the firm (urban or agricultural) and the individual and market equilibrium are made compatible. Though the full implications will not be made clear until chapter 5, these conditions have already been mentioned above. In the case of agriculture, a change in the price of the commodity will change the relevant bid-rent function, and the over-all market quantity adjustments are effected through the unlimited entry or exit of agricultural entrepreneurs in the market. However, since agricultural profits are held constant at "normal" for the entire range of bid rent curves, farmers have no preference among the curves. On the other hand, in our model of the urban market we shall assume the population of the city as given, and therefore the entry or exit of residential consumers will not be a variable for market equilibrium. The adjustment will take place through the individual's preference for lower bid price curves, which give him greater satisfaction. The case of the urban firm is intermediate. We shall consider a given number of firms, however large. Some of these may decline to enter the market if they cannot do so at a profit; that is to say, they will not enter the market unless they can bid successfully for land while staying below their zero-profits bid price curve. Thus, in the case of the urban firm, there is a limited entry and exit in the market. As in the case of the residential consumer, equilibria of the market and the unit will be brought into agreement through the firm's preference for lower bid price curves which enable it to realize larger profits. Column (8) merely indicates that in all cases, the farmer, the resident, and the urban firm, are indifferent along any given bid price or rent curve.

5

Market Equilibrium

A. INTRODUCTION

In this chapter an equilibrium solution will be presented for the land market of a city and its surrounding countryside. The location and the size of the site occupied by residents, urban firms, and agriculture will be determined by the use of bid price and bid rent curves.

The equilibrium requirements of the land market are similar to those of the market for any other good. At equilibrium, supply and demand quantities as well as prices must be equal. However, in the land market there are two goods (land and distance) but only one transaction and one price (that of land); therefore, the simple requirement of the equation of supply and demand prices and quantities becomes much more complicated.

Let us first examine the price relation. Every user of land, whether a resident, an urban firm, or a farmer, determines his location by the point of tangency of the lowest of his bid price curves[1] to come in contact with the price structure. Thus, at least one of the bid price curves of each user of land is in contact with the price structure. On the other hand, no equilibrium bid price curve can rise above the price structure, for if it did, the equilibrium bid price curve of that user would be a lower one.[2] The price structure is, therefore, the least upper bound of the equilibrium bid price curves of the users of land. As their name implies, the equilibrium bid price curves are the demand price; their envelope, the price structure, is the supply price. The equation of supply and demand prices for the land market consists of two parts: (1) the structure must be the envelope of the equilibrium bid price curves of the users of land, and (2) the

---

1. The verbal distinction between bid price and bid rent curves will not be continued; hereafter both shall be referred to as bid price curves.

2. From the definition of the equilibrium bid price curve, which is the lowest curve of the user's family of curves to come in contact with the price structure.

equilibrium bid price curve of every user of land must touch the price structure at one or more points, from the conditions of individual equilibrium.

For the market to be in equilibrium it is necessary that supply and demand quantities also be equated and that the market be cleared. That is to say, all of the land up to the edge of settlement must be sold, and no more land can be sold at a given distance than is available at that distance. This second is a logical requirement for consistency: clearly, no more of a good (land at a given location) can be sold than there is to sell. The requirement that all of the land up to the edge of settlement be sold stems from each landlord's desire to maximize his revenue, under the assumptions of sufficient knowledge of the market and no speculation. An unsold piece of land within the city produces no revenue for its landlord. Since the lot is within the city, it is preferable to the land at the edge of the city and should be able to command a price greater than zero. The landlord therefore should obtain some revenue greater than zero. The requirement of the equation of supply and demand quantities may be summarized as (1) compactness and (2) no overlap.

When these price and quantity conditions are met, there is market equilibrium. Put another way, the market will be in equilibrium when (1) no user of land can increase his profits or satisfaction by moving to some other location or by buying more or less land and (2) no landlord can increase his revenue by changing the price of his land.

The method of solution which will be presented below is very similar to the method used to solve for the agricultural land market. But there are differences which complicate the analysis, and a detailed explanation is necessary. We shall start with some simple game-like problems, from which the consideration of equilibrium quantities has been abstracted that we may consider the price relations by themselves. This type of solution will then be generalized, and the consideration of quantities will be reintroduced for a complete solution.

B. Simple Game Solutions[3]

We shall begin with a simple four-person game. There exists an

3. These problems will not be presented in terms of formal game theory, though the language will be similar.

unlimited supply of land at each of two locations, t_1 and t_2, where t_2 is the more distant location. These two plots are held respectively by landlords L_1 and L_2. Each of these will seek to maximize the price of his land,[4] but will not collude with the other. They will auction their land to the two other players, an urban resident, i, who seeks to maximize his satisfaction, and a farmer, ag. The farmer is willing to pay price p_{ag} at either or both locations. Either location may be occupied by either the farmer or the urban resident, but not by both. The solution of the game consists of finding where i and ag will locate, and the price at each location. The reader is referred to Figure 26.

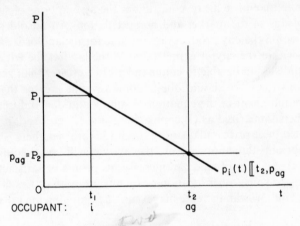

FIGURE 26. A four-person location game

It can be easily shown that i will locate at t_1 and ag at t_2. Since the farmer is willing to pay p_{ag} at either or both locations, i will have to bid and pay at least this price to have a place to live. But, as the individual prefers the nearer location t_1, he will always bid a higher price at t_1 than at t_2. Consequently a solution that has i at t_2 is impossible, for if i is at t_2, where he must pay at least p_{ag}, he would be willing to pay a higher price at t_1, where the price bid by the

4. The requirement that landlords seek to maximize price rather than revenue, as well as the assumption of an unlimited supply of land at each location, are used here as simplifying devices to avoid considering the quantities of land. The full method of solution presented in the concluding sections of this chapter will determine distances and quantities within the model in such a way that the landlords' goal is the same whether viewed as price or revenue maximization.

farmer is only p_{ag}. In such a case, neither would i have maximized his satisfaction (he could increase it by bidding a slightly higher price at t_1) nor would L_1 have maximized his price.

We know, then, that i will locate at t_1, and that ag will locate at t_2, paying p_{ag} to L_2. The one remaining question is what price, P_1, i will pay to L_1. We may start by setting a range. The price at t_1, P_1, must be at least equal to p_{ag}, so that $P_1 \geqslant p_{ag}$. On the other hand, the individual i would not be willing to pay a price higher than his bid price at t_1, using t_2, p_{ag} as the referee: $p_i(t_1)[\![t_2, p_{ag}$. For if P_1 were higher, the individual would increase his satisfaction by locating at t_2 and paying there a price equal to or slightly higher than p_{ag}. Consequently,

$$p_{ag} \leqslant P_1 \leqslant p_i(t_1)[\![t_2, p_{ag}.$$

This range can be reduced to an equality by considering the bargaining positions of i and L_1. By definition of the bid price curve, i receives equal or greater satisfaction at t_1 than at t_2 (at p_{ag}) as long as he pays a price within this range. Therefore, L_1 can charge any price within the range without fear of losing his high-paying tenant to L_2. Since L_1 wants to maximize his price, he will choose the extreme point of the range, and we may say that

$$P_1 = p_i(t_1)[\![t_2, p_{ag}.$$

thus completing the solution.[5]

A very similar solution would be found if the game were expanded to include more players. Consider two additional locations, t_3 and t_4, as in Figure 27, with their respective landlords L_3 and L_4. Consider as well an urban firm, f, and allow the farmer a sloped bid rent function, $p_{ag}(t)$, determined by the price of the agricultural commodity at the market. The price of the agricultural commodity is such that the farmer can pay no rent at t_4 after paying production and transportation costs; that is, $p_{ag}(t_4)=0$.

Rather than go through the verbally complicated mechanics of finding a solution, let the reader examine the solution presented in Figure 27. The farmer has located at t_3 and t_4, where he pays

5. It might be argued that i might bluff, or at any rate make bids at lower prices. However, we are assuming perfect knowledge of the market by the participants, so that bluffing will be unsuccessful, and L_1 will present counteroffers up to this maximum, secure in the knowledge that i has no more satisfactory choice.

$p_{ag}(t_3)$ and $p_{ag}(t_4)=0$ respectively.[6] Individual i has settled at t_2 where he pays a price P_2 determined by the price at t_3, $P_3 = p_{ag}(t_3)$. The relation is determined by i's bid price curve through t_3, P_3; that is, $P_2 = p_i(t_2)[\![t_3, P_3$. The firm, f, is located at t_1, where it pays a price P_1 determined by its bid price curve passing through t_2, P_2; that is, $P_1 = p_f(t_1)[\![t_2, P_2.$[7]

We have satisfied the requirement that supply and demand price be equal in that (1) at every point (t_1, t_2, t_3, t_4) at which the price structure has been defined (P_1, P_2, P_3, P_4), it is the least upper bound of the equilibrium bid price curves of the consumers of land

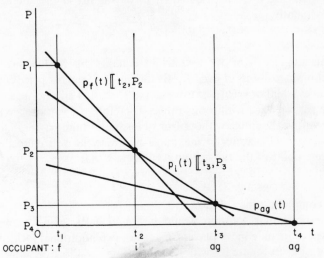

FIGURE 27. A seven-person-location game

(p_{ag}, p_i, p_f); and (2) each of the bid price curves comes in contact with the price structure at least once. Put another way, no consumer can reach a lower bid price curve (increase his profit or satisfaction) by moving to another location, and no landlord can increase his price without losing his customer.[8] It should be noted that this price

6. It does not matter whether the farmer produces at t_4. In either case, the rent there will be zero.

7. There is a possible exception, but it does not affect the argument. See appendix I, note 1.

8. If the price P_1 is increased at t_1, f moves to t_2; if P_2 is increased, i moves to t_3; and if P_3 or P_4 are increased, the farmer ceases to operate at that location.

structure (P_1, P_2, P_3, P_4), while it satisfies the equilibrium requirements, is discontinuous.

The essential point to be grasped from the market solution of these simple games is that price at any location is related to the prices at the other locations by means of the bid price curves of the users of land. The price paid by a user at his equilibrium location is equal to the value at that location of his bid price curve defined by the price at his next most preferred location. More formally, the price P_i paid by an individual i at his equilibrium location t_i will be —when his next most preferred location is t_j at price P_j:

$$P_i = p_i(t_i)[\![t_j, P_j.$$

If it were greater, individual i would move to t_j; if it were less, the landlord at t_i would not be realizing the full advantage of his location. The difference between the prices at the equilibrium location and at the location used as a referee is the location or situation differential rent which economists since Ricardo have recognized.[9] The price and location used as a referee shall be called a marginal price and marginal location, or marginal price-location.

The price for land paid by a user at his equilibrium location is determined by his bid price curve passing through his marginal price-location. But this user's marginal price-location will be some other user's equilibrium price-location. Thus, the whole price structure consists of a chain of equilibrium and marginal price-location pairs, both points of each pair lying within the equilibrium bid price curve of the same user. If we knew the location of each user, and his marginal location, we could form the chain of the price structure link by link from the bid price mappings of the users, provided we knew the price at any one location (for instance, the price of agricultural land at the edge of the urban sector, or the price—zero—at the margin of the economy as a whole). Conceivably, one might try all the possible permutations of users and locations, and see which would satisfy the equilibrium conditions. But the number of permutations rises with the square of the factorial of the number of users, and the problem would rapidly become unmanageable. However, it is possible to derive a method to

9. See appendix I, note 2 for the relation of the model to several rent concepts that frequently appear in the literature of economics: economic rent, opportunity costs, location differential rent.

assign the users to their respective locations from an examination of their bid price mappings and it is possible to make a generalization on the spatial relationship of marginal and equilibrium price-locations. The next section will be devoted to finding such a method and such a generalization.

C. Spatial Sequence of Users of Land and Marginal and Equilibrium Price-Location Pairs

In this section we wish to find a method of establishing a chain of pairs of marginal and equilibrium price-locations that will include all users of land. Since the method is of necessity cumbersome, it may help the reader to anticipate the conclusions. These are, in brief:

(1) in general, the steeper his bid price curve, the nearer the center of the city will a user of land locate;

(2) in general, the marginal price-location of a user of land is the equilibrium price-location of the user immediately in back of him (away from the center); and, conversely, the equilibrium price of a user is equal to the bid price for that location (marginal price) of the user immediately in front of him.

These conclusions are based on well-behaved curves; very irregular curves require adjustments in the method of solution.

It may also help the reader to have a more human interpretation of these conclusions. It will be remembered that for the residential consumer the slope of the bid price curve is determined by the shape of the indifference surface and by the marginal costs of commuting (see Figure 23). The shape of the indifference surface is a representation of the individual's tastes. The faster this surface moves up and away from the t-axis, the more compensation the individual requires for the nuisance of commuting, and the steeper the bid price curve becomes. Thus, the steepness of the bid price curve may be viewed as an indication of how much the individual cares to be near the center in order to avoid commuting, and it is reasonable to expect that an individual with a steep curve will outbid an individual with a gentler one for central locations.

The interpretation of the slope of the bid price curve of the firm is similar (see equation (3:14), chapter 3). The steepness of the slope is determined by the rate at which sales drop and costs increase with increasing distance from the center (excluding consideration of site size in the denominator). Firms with a rapid drop in sales and increase in costs will bid more aggressively for central locations.

Spatial Sequence and Steepness of the Bid Price Curves

In this section we shall show that the users of land with steeper curves locate more centrally.

Consider individual i at his equilibrium location, t_i, where he pays price P_i (see Figure 28). His equilibrium bid price curve is $p_i(t)[\![t_i, P_i$, which we will denote for simplicity as $p_i(t)$. Consider as

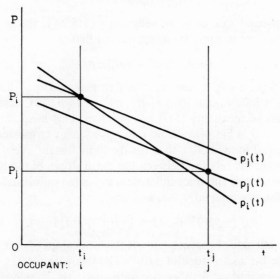

FIGURE 28. Diagram for the proof of the relation of the steepness of bid price curves to centrality of location

well another individual, j, whose equilibrium location is at a greater distance t_j (that is, $t_i < t_j$), where he pays price P_j. His equilibrium bid price curve is $p_j(t)[\![t_j, P_j$, which will be denoted as $p_j(t)$. Since these individuals are in equilibrium, their equilibrium bid price curves can nowhere be above the price structure. Therefore we may say that:

(5:1) $$p_i(t_j) \leqslant P_j$$

(5:2) $$p_j(t_i) \leqslant P_i.$$

By definition, at the equilibrium location, equilibrium bid price and the actual price are equal:

(5:3) $$p_i(t_i) = P_i$$

(5:4) $$p_j(t_j) = P_j.$$

Subtracting equation (5:3) from inequality (5:1), and inequality (5:2) from equation (5:4), we obtain:

(5:5) $$p_i(t_j) - p_i(t_i) \leqslant P_j - P_i$$

(5:6) $$p_j(t_j) - p_j(t_i) \geqslant P_j - P_i.$$

The right-hand side of both inequalities (5:5, 6) is the same. The inequalities are in opposite directions, so that:

(5:7) $$p_i(t_j) - p_i(t_i) \leqslant p_j(t_j) - p_j(t_i).$$

Since bid price curves are negatively sloped, and t_j is the greater distance, it follows that $p_i(t_i) > p_i(t_j)$ and $p_j(t_i) > p_j(t_j)$. Consequently both sides of inequality (5:7) are negative. This inequality states that the drop in bid prices from t_i to t_j is as great or greater for the more central individual, i, than for the more distant one, j.

To obtain the relation between the mean slopes of the bid price curves, we divide the price differences indicated in inequality (5:7) by the distance interval, $t_j - t_i$, and obtain:

$$[p_i(t_j) - p_i(t_i)]/(t_j - t_i) \leqslant [p_j(t_j) - p_j(t_i)]/(t_j - t_i).$$

Now the left side of the inequality is the mean slope of $p_i(t)$, and the right side the mean slope of $p_j(t)$.[10] The inequality states, that, in the distance interval between two individuals, the individual nearer the center will have an equilibrium bid price curve at least as steep on the average as the farther individual's.[11]

Note that what we have just proved applies to average steepness; we have not proved that the bid price curves are steeper at every point. Note also that this does not mean that the price structure need be convex toward the center (that it must be steeper near the center). If the bid price curves of the various users are concave

10. Note that the limit of this inequality, as $(t_j - t_i) \to 0$ is $dp_i/dt \leqslant dp_j/dt$.

11. The bid price curve of j through i's equilibrium price location will also be less steep than i's equilibrium bid price curve; i's bid price curve through j's equilibrium price-location will be steeper than j's equilibrium curve. See appendix I, note 3 for the formal proof.

toward the center, the price structure may also be concave, though less so.

Marginal and Equilibrium Price-Location Pairs for Bid Price Curves of Constant Ranking by Steepness

In this section we shall find that the marginal price-location of any user of land will be the equilibrium location of the individual directly in back of him. We shall prove this only for curves that maintain a constant ranking by steepness at every point. That is to say, the curves must satisfy the condition that if we consider the slopes of the bid price curves of users h, i, j at any price location, we shall always find, for instance, that h's curve is steeper than i's, which is a steeper curve than j's (that is, $dp_h/dt < dp_i/dt < dp_j/dt$). We shall postpone consideration of curves which do not maintain this constant ranking until section E of this chapter.

We shall use the method of *reductio ad absurdum*. Assume that the marginal price-location of individual h's is not i's equilibrium price-location, t_i, P_i, which is directly in back of h, but a more distant t_j, P_j. That is,

$$(5:8) \qquad t_h < t_i < t_j.$$

We have just proved that the more centrally located users of land have steeper bid price curves. We are assuming a constant ranking in steepness of the bid price curves, so that at every point:

$$(5:9) \qquad dp_h/dt < dp_i/dt < dp_j/dt.$$

We are saying that h, at an equilibrium price-location t_h, P_h, has a marginal price-location t_j, P_j. By definition, both the marginal and the equilibrium price locations of a user of land are on his equilibrium bid price curve. Therefore,

$$(5:10) \qquad P_j = p_h(t_j)[\![t_h, P_h.$$

On the other hand, we are saying that the intermediate location t_i at price P_i is not marginal, so that

$$(5:11) \qquad P_i > p_h(t_i)[\![t_h, P_h.$$

But now consider the bid price curve of i through his own equilibrium price-location, $p_i(t)[\![t_i, P_i.$ Since, from inequality (5:9), this curve is less steep than h's equilibrium curve, and, since, by inequality (5:11), it lies above h's equilibrium bid price curve at t_i, it follows that

$$(5:12) \qquad p_i(t_j)[\![t_i, P_i > P_j.$$

But if inequality (5:12) is true, then the price structure is not an upper bound of the equilibrium bid price curves, and the market is not in equilibrium. Consequently, where the ranking by steepness of the bid price curves is constant, the marginal price-location of h must be the location immediately in back of its equilibrium price-location.

We have assumed that the marginal price-location had to be to the rear, away from the center of the city, of the equilibrium location. We have proved that if it is to the rear, it must be adjacent. Had we assumed it to be to the front, toward the center, we could have demonstrated that the marginal price-location had to be adjacent in front by a similar proof. Therefore, while it is clear that the marginal location is adjacent to the equilibrium one, it is not clear whether it will be to the front or to the rear. Let us examine both possibilities, which are illustrated in Figures 29 and 30. For

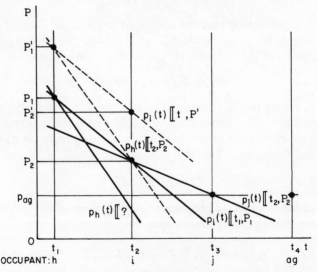

FIGURE 29. Instability of a price structure based on front marginal price-locations

simplicity, only three individuals are used, h, i, j, in addition to an agricultural demand bidding at a constant price, p_{ag}. Figure 29 shows a front marginal price-location, and Figure 30 a rear one.

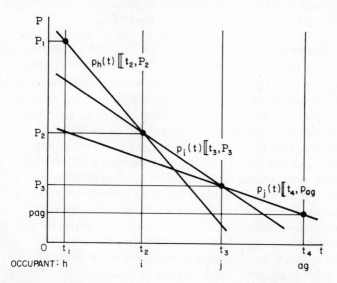

FIGURE 30. A stable price structure based on rear marginal price-locations

In Figure 29, the marginal price-location of j is t_2, P_2, and that of i, t_1, P_1. But h has no marginal price-location at all. The landlord at that location could raise the price at that location up to $P'_1 = p_h(t_1)[\![t_2, P_2$ before h would find t_2, P_2 preferable. This, in turn, would increase i's marginal price to P'_1, thus increasing the price he must pay at t_2 to P'_2. This increase in price at t_2 would enable the landlord at t_1 to raise his price again, and the process would be explosive. The same situation would apply to individual j at t_3 with respect to his marginal price at t_2.

The explosion is limited, however, because, at some point, individual j at t_3 would find location t_4 at p_{ag} preferable to t_2 at a higher price. He would then shift his reference (marginal price-location) from the front to the rear. Similarly, at some level of prices, every individual in the chain would find the rear location preferable as a margin. Thus, Figure 30, with a rear marginal price-location, may be regarded as the limit which a situation as in

Figure 29 would reach. Figure 30 represents a stable solution, where no landlord can raise his price without losing his customer, and no individual has any inducement to change his location. Therefore, in a market solution, the marginal price-location for each user of land will be the location directly in back of him.[12]

D. GENERALIZED GAME EQUILIBRIUM SOLUTION FOR BID PRICE CURVES WITH A CONSTANT RANKING BY STEEPNESS

We are now in a position to generalize the solution of games such as those presented in section B. In these games we are given the bid price curve mapping for every potential user of land (and these mappings conform to the constant ranking by steepness requirement); we are also given all possible locations and the price of land at any one location. Typically the price known will be that at the margin of the system. If agriculture is considered in the system, this price will be zero. If we are considering only the urban sector, the price of land at the margin will be the price bid by agriculture at that location. If there are n users of land in the game, the marginal location will be t_{n+1}, and its price P_{n+1}.[13]

In section C we showed that the individual or firm with the least steep bid price curve will settle farthest from the center. The user of land with the least steep bid price curves will settle at the last occupied or nth location, t_n, directly in front of t_{n+1}. He will be denominated by the letter n. His marginal price location will be t_{n+1}, P_{n+1}, and he will pay a price P_n at t_n determined by his bid price curve through this marginal location:

$$P_n = p_n(t_n)[\![t_{n+1}, P_{n+1}.$$

The next individual toward the center will be the one with the next least steep bid price curves. He will be called $n-1$. His location, one step closer to the center than t_n, will be t_{n-1}. He will pay a price P_{n-1}, determined by his bid price curve with reference to his marginal price-location, t_n, P_n:

$$P_{n-1} = p_{n-1}(t_{n-1})[\![t_n, P_n.$$

12. There exists a case in which a user who had an extremely sharp break in the slope of his bid price curve might arrive at a stable front marginal price-location. The case is examined in appendix I, note 5, but it is merely a theoretical curiosity.

13. See below for the possibility that some firms will decline to enter the market. In that case, the number $(n+1)$ would diminish by the number of firms which decline to enter.

Thus, the chain is formed, link by link, until the price paid by the user with the steepest bid price curves at the center of the city is established.

In general, then, we are given the locations $(t_1, t_2, \ldots, t_{n+1})$ and the marginal price of the market (P_{n+1}), the market equilibrium solution is given by:

$$P_n = p_n(t_n)[\![t_{n+1}, P_{n+1}$$

$$P_{n-1} = p_{n-1}(t_{n-1})[\![t_n, P_n$$

$$\cdot$$
$$\cdot$$
$$\cdot$$

$$P_i = p_i(t_i)[\![t_{i+1}, P_{i+1}$$

$$\cdot$$
$$\cdot$$
$$\cdot$$

$$P_1 = p_1(t_1)[\![t_2, P_2 ;$$

where
$$\frac{d}{dt}p_i(t)[\![t_k, P_k < \frac{d}{dt}p_{i+1}(t)[\![t_k, P_k$$

$$i = 1, 2, \ldots, (n-1)$$

$$t_i < t_{i+1} \quad \text{any } t_k, P_k.$$

Since each firm has a highest bid price curve (where profits are zero), it may be that some firms cannot make successful bids at any locations. Then, in solving, we may run out of bidders before the central location is reached. In that case, if w firms have declined to enter the market, the solution should be tried again with a market margin at t_{n+1-w}, at the corresponding marginal price P_{n+1-w}. This will yield a lower price structure at which some of these w firms may now choose to enter the market, so that we have more bidders than locations. A new marginal location should be chosen to accommodate these, and the solution tried again. A few iterations (no more than $w-1$) will disclose the correct number of bidders and the marginal price-location.

E. Game Equilibrium Solution when Bid Price Curves do not Maintain a Constant Ranking in their Steepness

The method outlined in the preceding section was based on the assumption that the bid price curves retained a constant ranking in their steepness. This is a strong assumption, not likely to be met in reality. Slight departures from this will not be important, but bid price curves which differ significantly in shape will require adjustments in the method of solution.

The slope, and thus the shape, of bid price curves are ultimately determined by the tastes of the individual.[14] We may expect that the curves of individuals of different tastes will differ in their shape. It will be remembered from chapter 4 that the slope of a bid price curve may be equated roughly to the added (marginal) expense and bother of commuting as distance from the center increases. Thus, an individual who does not mind walking may be expected to have a gently sloped bid price curve up to the limit of what he considers walking distance; if he dislikes other means of transportation, beyond this limit his curve will be fairly steep. His bid price curve would look like $p_i(t)$ in Figure 31, where t_0 is the limit of his walking range. On the other hand, an individual who detests walking and insists on driving everywhere will have decreasing increments in nuisance and expense as distance increases. His bid price curve may be shaped like curve $p_j(t)$ in Figure 31. Curve $p_j(t)$ is steeper than $p_i(t)$ up to t_0, but thereafter it is less steep.

The possible shapes of the bid price curves are unlimited, even though the preference for near locations guarantees a negative slope. The procedure for market solution for curves of constant ranking by steepness may be preserved in the case of curves of varying shapes, though with some modifications to be presented below. This will minimize the possibility of an erroneous solution from irregularly shaped curves. However, no method was found to handle every possible case in a systematic way, and some elements of error may be present in the solution. These would have to be corrected by trial and error—"by hand"—in a series of iterations after inspecting the first solution.

We shall assume that a large number of people have similar

14. Only the factors influencing the shape of residential bid price curves are discussed here. The factors affecting commercial curves will be parallel.

tastes, and therefore similarly shaped bid price curves, for which the assumption of constant ranking by steepness would hold approximately. The shape of the bid price curve of one of these individuals may be thought of as being "normal," and used as the basis of comparison for irregularly shaped bid price curves. The two simplest cases of irregular curves, then, would be that of a curve more concave to the origin (e.g., $p_i(t)$ in Figure 31) and that of a curve more convex to the origin (e.g., $p_j(t)$ in Figure 31) than the "normal"

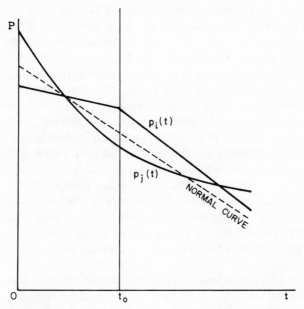

FIGURE 31. Diagrammatic bid price curves of individuals of different tastes

curve.[15] Below is a summary of the principal problems encountered when dealing with such curves. A fuller analysis is presented in appendix I, notes 4, 5, and 6.

15. In Figure 31 the normal curve has been shown as a straight line to make the convexity or concavity of the other curves clearer. This does not mean, of course, that such a normal curve need be straight. The comparisons of concavity and convexity with regard to some curved normal curve could be made either through the mathematical definition of curvature or by means of some transformation of the t-axis such that the normal curve appeared as a straight line.

Convex Curves

By comparison to the normal curve, a curve convex to the origin is steeper nearer the center of the city and less steep farther out. As a consequence, should one compare the steepnesses of the bid price curves of the various potential users at the margin of the system, such a curve would appear to be among the least steep. However, near the center of the city, the convex curve might be among the steepest. If the procedure outlined for curves of constant ranking by steepness is followed, this user would be assigned to a distant location. This would not lead to error if the convexity were slight. However, if the convexity is fairly sharp, the steepness of the curve near the center of the city would preponderate, and the correct location for this user would be a more central one. If instead of comparing the slopes of the bid price curves at the periphery, we do so at every location, beginning with the central one, this greater steepness of convex curves will be recognized, and most users with convex curves will be properly situated. The reason for the advantage of starting at the center of the city rather than at the periphery in comparing the steepness of bid price curves is that, since distance from the center is inversely related to steepness of the bid price curves, the price structure resulting from a market solution will itself be more convex than the normal bid price curve. Consequently, the steeper part of a convex bid price curve is likely to be of greater importance, while the part of the curve which is less steep will probably be subsumed in the decreasing steepness of the price structure.

A second characteristic of convex bid price curves is that, for very convex curves, there may be several intermediate occupants of land between the equilibrium and marginal price-locations. Extremely convex curves will correspond to locations either at the center or on the extreme periphery.

See appendix I, note 4 for a fuller discussion of convex curves.

Concave Curves

Bid price curves concave to the origin present less of a problem than convex curves. Since the price structure will itself be more convex than the normal bid price curves, concave curves will not rise above it. Concave curves appear less steep near the center of the city, and steeper toward the periphery. Consequently, a comparison of the steepness of the bid price curves of the various potential users at either the center or the periphery will be a poor indicator of the correct location of the user with concave bid price curves. The problem can be easily solved by comparing the steepness of the bid price curves starting at either extreme and comparing the steepness of the curves of the unallocated users at each location in succession. The user with concave curves will locate where his curve is the least steep (of the unallocated curves) if one has started from the periphery, or where it is the steepest (of the unallocated curves) if one has started from the center of the city.

See appendix I, note 5 for a fuller discussion of concave curves.

Mixed Curves

We have just examined convex and concave curves as the two simplest cases of departure from a normal curve. They are simple because they have a single bend or twist. Yet tastes can vary in such ways that it is possible for a bid price curve to have many twists, being now concave and now convex. There are infinite shapes possible for such mixed curves, and no all-purpose systematic treatment has been found to handle them. All that can be suggested is that the system be solved as far as possible on the assumption of constant ranking by steepness of the bid price curves, with the precautions just mentioned for simple concave and convex curves. Then adjustments should be made where necessary for the more complicated curves according to the ingenuity of the solver. One such method for making adjustments is presented in appendix I, note 6. The situation is analogous to that encountered when one tries to integrate a function. Some simple functions can be integrated in a systematic way; other functions belong to recognizable types which can be integrated more or less systematically; but there remain others for which no system exists, and in these cases the solution depends on the ingenuity and powers of observation of those attempting the solution.

Summary of Procedure for Curves which do not maintain a Constant Ranking in their Steepness

We have proved that the bid price curves of the individuals nearer the center of the city must have a greater mean steepness than those of individuals farther away. This relationship of averages must hold in an equilibrium solution, regardless of the shape of the bid price curves. When we are trying to find an equilibrium solution for users of land whose bid price curves do not maintain a constant ranking in their steepness, we make a series of educated guesses about these average relationships. The method of solution is rendered less susceptible to error (1) by starting at the central location (this reduces the likelihood of errors arising from convex curves); and (2) by comparing the steepness of curves at each successive location (this reduces the likelihood of error from both concave and convex curves). Ultimately, however, the shapes of the bid price curves may be such that errors remain and the solution obtained must be tested to insure the price structure is truly the envelope of the bid price curves. If it is not, further adjustments are necessary which cannot be completely systematized.

F. Clearance of the Market:
Solution considering Quantities

In the previous sections we have presented a solution for a strange sort of market. In the first place, the possible locations were given. This is not a reasonable assumption for the featureless plain on which our assumed city sits. It would be desirable to view all locations as possible along the continuous dimension of distance from the center, and to arrive at the actual locations of the firms and individuals through the mechanism of the market. A second deficiency has been that the suppliers (landlords) have sought to maximize price, rather than the more reasonable goal of maximizing revenue. A third deficiency, closely related to the second, was that we avoided the problem of equating supply and demand quantities. The firm or consumer who bid the highest price at a location could buy as much or as little land as he wished at that location. Thus, we assumed an inexhaustible supply of land at each location and avoided the consideration of supply quantities by having the landlord maximize price rather than revenue. In this section these deficiencies of the model will be remedied by introducing a relatively slight complication.

A fourth deficiency will remain, however. The two-dimensional plain of the city has been simplified to a single dimension (distance from the center). We shall simplify into a pattern of concentric rings the complicated mosaic of essentially rectangular lots that exists in reality. To have more realistically shaped lots would complicate the analysis out of all proportion (see appendix B). The effect of this simplification, however, is slight, and will be discussed further in section G.

Determination of Distances within the Model

First, let us try to fix the distances of the various locations, t_1, t_2, et cetera, within the model. To do this, let us define a function $S(t)$, where $S(t_i)$ is the total amount of land enclosed by a circle of radius t_i, with the center at the core of the city. In a featureless plain, $S(t)$ will be in the form of the area of the circle: $S(t) = \pi t^2$. However, if some of this area is not available for urban or agricultural land use, as in the case of portions covered by water or reserved for non-competing land uses such as parks, institutions, or streets, then almost any form of the function $S(t)$ is possible, as long as $S(t) \leqslant \pi t^2$. From the point of view of market equilibrium the function $S(t)$ is known: it is obtained from the measurement of areas from a map.

By definition, the most central location available to the competing bidders for land is t_1, where $S(t_1) = 0$. The user of land with the steepest bid price curves will locate at t_1. In the case of a featureless plain, $t_1 = 0$, but if there is a historic or government center at the geometric center, t_1 may be some greater distance.

The user of land which locates next closest to the center will take the next available location, t_2. This distance can be found by discovering the first available location after the wants of the first individual are satisfied. If we know P_1,[16] the price at t_1, we can find the quantity of land, q_1, which the individual or the firm which locates there will buy (by the method of partial solution for land when distance is known, as in chapter 2). Then the second location can be found by solving for t_2 in

$$S(t_2) = q_1.$$

The price P_2 at t_2 can be found from the first user's bid price curve

16. Allow this assumption for the moment, it will be discussed further below.

mapping. P_2, t_2 is in all likelihood the marginal price-location of the first user,[17] so that

$$P_2 = p_1(t_2)[\![t_1, P_1.$$

By finding the quantity of land, q_2, demanded by the second user, we can determine the third location by solving for t_3 in

$$S(t_3) = q_1 + q_2.$$

The price P_3 at t_3 will be the marginal price of individual 2:

$$P_3 = p_2(t_3)[\![t_2, P_2.$$

In general, we may solve for the location of the ith user of land by solving for t_i in

$$S(t_i) = \sum_{j=1}^{i-1} q_j,$$

where the subscripts denominate the users of land by their closeness to the center. And we can solve for the price P_i at location t_i by the chain of equilibrium and marginal price locations, the last link of which will be the marginal price of i's nearest neighbor toward the center

$$P_i = p_{i-1}(t_i)[\![t_{i-1}, P_{i-1}.$$

The distance to the edge of settlement, t_{n+1},[18] where there are n consumers of land, will be

$$S(t_{n+1}) = \sum_{i=1}^{n} q_i.$$

This merely states that the total area covered by the land uses considered will be equal to the sum of the individual lots.

The price of land at the edge of settlement can be calculated from the last link of the chain of equilibrium and marginal price-locations:

$$P_{n+1} = p_n(t_{n+1})[\![t_n, P_n.$$

17. In accordance with the preceding section, if the analysis of the chain of equilibrium and marginal price-locations is started from the center, the chance of error from irregular curves is diminished. There remains some possibility of error, however. If the conditions of market equilibrium are not satisfied in a solution by this method, the process should be repeated after corrections in the manner outlined in the preceding section.

18. If the level of land prices is such that some of the firms decline to enter, the ordinal subscript will be reduced accordingly. However, in this case, where we are solving from the center outward, there will be no need to iterate to find the correct ordinal at the margin of the market.

On the other hand, this final marginal price will be independently known,[19] and the agreement between the calculated and the given marginal price will be a necessary condition for a correct solution. It will be remembered that we began the chain by assuming a certain price P_1 at the center of the city. The marginal price, P_{n+1}, arrived at after following the chain, will depend on the assumed central price. The correct value of P_1 is that which will yield, as a result of the chain of equilibrium and marginal price-locations, a marginal price P_{n+1} which is exactly equal to the given price at that location (be it zero or the agricultural price). If the central price P_1 is assumed too high, the whole chain will be too high, and the calculated marginal price will be greater than the given one. The solution should then be tried again with a lower estimated price at the center. The opposite will obtain if P_1 is assumed too low. Successive iterations with lower or higher estimated prices at the center will result in successive approximations to the correct solution. The iterations should be continued until a satisfactory number of significant figures has been obtained. Alternatively, after the first approximation has yielded the spatial sequence of the users of land, it would be possible to use the method described in the appendix A.

The iterative process is summarized and stated more formally in Table 2.

Supply and Demand Quantities and the Maximization of Suppliers' Revenue

We have modified the model to have distances determined within it. In doing this we have also solved the problems of equating supply and demand quantities and of having the supplier maximize revenue rather than price.

Clearance of the market as a whole, with respect to quantities, is expressed in the relation

$$S(t_{n+1}) = \sum_{j=1}^{n} q_j;$$

where the left side of the equation represents the supply quantity

19. If we are considering urban firms, residents, and agriculture, the marginal price of the land market will be zero, since the location is unoccupied. If only the urban sector is considered (firms and residences), the marginal location t_{n+1}, will be occupied by agriculture, and the marginal price will be that bid by agriculture at that location.

TABLE 2. Steps for the derivation of market equilibrium

STEP	PRICE CALCULATED FROM	LOCATION CALCULATED FROM	SIZE OF SITE*
(1)	P_1 = estimated	t_1 = given	
(2)			q_1
(3)		$S(t_2) = q_1$	
(4)	$P_2 = p_1(t_2) \llbracket t_1, P_1$		
(5)			q_2
(6)		$S(t_3) = q_1 + q_2$	
(3_{i-2})		$S(t_i) = \sum_{j=1}^{i-1} q_j$	
(3_{i-1})	$P_i = p_{i-1}(t_i) \llbracket t_{i-1}, P_{i-1}$		
(3_i)			q_i
		$S(t_{n+1}) = \sum_{j=1}^{n} q_j$	
(3_{n+2})	$P_{n+1} = p_n(t_{n+1}) \llbracket t_n, P_n$		

NOTE: Iterations by changing the estimated value of P_1 in the direction of the difference of the given minus the calculated values of P_{n+1}.

*Quantities of land calculated from the partial equilibrium solutions presented in chapters 2 and 3, since price and location are given. See W. Isard, *Location and Space Economy* and E. S. Dunn, *The Location of Agricultural Production* for the quantity of land of the agricultural firm.

and the right side the total demand quantity. That is to say, no land remains unsold within the city. The relation

$$q_j = S(t_{j+1}) - S(t_j)^{20}$$

insures that each user buys all of the land between his two adjacent neighbors and that there is no overlap of lots (that is, no more land is sold than there is available at any location).

Another by-product is that the suppliers have now maximized their revenue as well as their price. Any supplier holding a stock of land within the perimeter t_{n+1} will now have sold all his stock. Since he has maximized price and sold all his stock, he has maximized revenue as well.[21]

G. The Shape of the Lot

Our view of the individual lot as a thin ring around the center of the city is, of course, a shortcoming of the model just presented. It arises from our inability to handle the geometric complexities that would result from more realistically shaped lots. However, it also arises from a conceptual simplification implicit in the preceding discussion: the utility function of the individual and the cost and revenue equations for the firm allowed only for the quantity of land, but not for the shape of the lot.[22] Put another way, we are still plagued by the problem mentioned in the introductory chapter, that we are dealing with the user of land as if he located at a point, while the necessity of equating supply and demand quantities requires that we extend this point so that it will have an area (q). For this reason, the acceptability of the assumption of concentric lots must be examined further.

It was shown above[23] that $q_j = S(t_{j+1}) - S(t_j)$, so that a two-dimensional interpretation of the shape of the lot is a ring. However,

20. This is easily derived from the equations used to determine distance. Since

$$S(t_j) = \sum_{i=1}^{j-1} q_i \text{ and } S(t_{j+1}) = \sum_{i=1}^{j} q_i, \text{ then, by subtraction, } q_j = S(t_{j+1}) - S(t_j).$$

21. This assumes a plurality of landlords in competition with each other. If a single supplier held all the land, he might be able to devise some other price structure to maximize his revenue by considering price elasticities (and transport costs).

22. The manner in which the shape of the lot may be considered for the individual is described in appendix B.

23. See note 20.

it will be noted that nothing was said about j that made use of the annular shape of the lot. Our initial assumption is that user j will be located at the first location available after the quantities demanded by the more centrally located users have been supplied. This is expressed by the requirement $S(t_j) = \sum_{i=1}^{j-1} q_i$. It is only after looking at the next user, $j+1$, for whom $S(t_{j+1}) = \sum_{i=1}^{j} q_i$, that we deduce that j's lot is ring-shaped. In short, the doubtful requirement of ring-shaped lots is not assumed directly; it is, rather, a corollary of the reasonable requirement that a user shall not occupy land already occupied by others. It is a corollary that stems from the two-dimensional geometric interpretation of the quantitative statement $q_j = S(t_{j+1}) - S(t_j)$. Geometric interpretations require the attribute of shape as well as that of quantity, and the only two-dimensional interpretation of that quantitative statement is a ring. However, our model has been postulated in a one-dimensional geometry (the dimension of distance), so that it is not surprising that it should be deficient in this respect when interpreted in two dimensions. In brief, since the model has not been designed to answer questions as to the shape of the lot, its answers to these questions may be disregarded.

There is an alternative to trying to establish the shape of the lot. The reasonable requirement that the user not occupy land already occupied by those nearer the center may be viewed as a statistical statement, permitting lots to be of any shape as long as their sum (demand quantity) equals the land available to this distance from the center (supply quantity). The deduction that the lots are ring-shaped is not pursued, on the basis that the theory does not possess the degree of refinement requisite for establishing a precise shape for the "extended point" of the lot. This view would be acceptable, in particular, in operational statistical models, such as that discussed in chapter 6, which consider bid price curves and their associated quantities of land for groups of firms or individuals. Within these broader rings (and other shapes evolved from rings) individual lots may be of any shape.

6

Some Applications of the Model and an Outline for Empirical Research

A. INTRODUCTION

In the first five chapters we have developed a model of the land market of a city. In this chapter we shall put this model to various uses. We shall re-examine the "minimum costs of friction hypothesis" in the light of our theory. We shall also outline certain avenues for further research, with particular attention to empirical research. The presentation in this chapter will be less rigorously mathematical than in the development of the model. Particularly in the later sections, the discussion will be suggestive rather than exhaustive.

B. THE MINIMUM COSTS OF FRICTION HYPOTHESIS

In chapter 1 reference was made to R. Haig's hypothesis of minimum costs of friction and to its subsequent restatements.[1] This theory, in its original form, held that the operations of an urban land market, given free competition and perfect knowledge, would result in minimum aggregate land rents and transport costs for the city as a whole. Since then the theory has been restated in other ways to the effect that what is being minimized for the whole city is rents plus transport costs plus some form of disutility.[2] The inclusion of disutility may be sensible in terms of a broad definition of costs, but it robs the theory of strength. In the first place, you cannot add dollars and disutility, and the theory is placed beyond any hope of

---

1. See chapter 1, section C.
2. See in particular the quotation from Quinn in chapter 1. See also the quotations from the land economists in the same chapter.

empirical testing or even of precise, logical statements.[3] Moreover, there is the problem of aggregating the disutilities of different persons. It requires unbounded faith in the capabilities of the social sciences to believe that the driver's boredom, the subway-rider's claustrophobia, and the anxiety of the timid can be compounded into a common quantity, measured in units of whatever kind, of which we could say unequivocally that it is increasing or decreasing.[4] For these reasons, the minimum costs of friction hypothesis will be examined in its original strict formulation, where the costs of friction are only rents and transport costs.

The reader will remember that the minimum costs hypothesis was derived from the view, after von Thünen's analysis, that activities locate so as to minimize their costs of friction. Haig extended this view of the firm's behavior to the city as a whole, concluding that the sum of these minima would itself be a minimum.[5] However, it has been argued here, after Chamberlin and others, that the urban firm locates so as to maximize profits, and that the costs of friction are only one of the elements considered in balancing costs against revenues. Minimizing the costs of friction would be the criterion for location only in the special case where revenue and all other costs were constant. It should be remembered that Haig developed his theory from the consideration of the location of manufacturing firms, for which these conditions may be approximated in certain cases. Neither can residences be said to

3. The problem of addition of dissimilar units encountered in this case is insoluble. It should not be confused, however, with the use of utility functions and marginal rates of substitution. In this common usage, units of utility encounter other units (dollars, pounds, miles) only in terms of ratios (pure numbers). The ratios of marginal utilities (marginal rates of substitution) may be established empirically by revealed preferences. Wingo, in *Transportation and Urban Land*, adds the dollar value of time in travel (defined by the marginal value of leisure) to the costs of travel as such. However, this does not take into account tastes as such: traveling one hour in a crowded subway is viewed as equivalent to an hour traveled in an air-conditioned, chauffered limousine. It does not relate, moreover, the time or disutility of travel to the taste for land or for other goods, but rather defines travel time as being an addition to working hours, and prices it in relation to them. Residential location in Wingo's model is determined by the minimizing of transport costs (including time) plus rent, the two being arithmetic complements adding up to transport costs to the margin.

4. See also Paul A. Samuelson, "Social Indifference Curves," *Quart. Econ.*, 70:1 (Feb. 1956).

5. Wingo, in *Transportation and Urban Land*, argues similarly, but says only that the aggregate minimum seems probable by analogy.

locate so as to minimize the costs of friction. Rather, they seek to maximize satisfaction. The millionaire with an estate of several acres one hour away from the city could reduce his costs of friction by moving into a slum dwelling at the center of the city. In general, anyone could reduce the rent element of his costs of friction by being content with a smaller lot than that which he occupies. Consequently, the minimizing of the costs of friction are not a sufficient criterion for location either for residences or urban firms.

Having rejected the assumptions on which the minimum aggregate costs of friction hypothesis is based, we might reject the hypothesis out of hand. But, drawing a distinction between the theory as a statement of fact and the explanation of this fact, we must still see whether the hypothesis is valid, though we do not accept the premises. The hypothesis is important because Haig, and others after him, have seen in it a principle for city planning. The function of the planner, in this view, is to counterbalance the effects of the imperfections of the market, which increase friction, and to plan so that the costs of friction are minimized. Such costs are viewed as unproductive: the friction of moving about things and people, and the paying for a location so that they do not have to be moved farther.

The solution of a free market of urban land is a unique solution, both in the model presented in these pages and in the view of Haig and his disciples. The minimum aggregate costs of friction are thus not the low point of a continuous function, but a unique value, once the "rules of the game" are given. They will be a minimum compared to the costs of friction under alternative institutional conditions or given certain realistic imperfections of the market. The number of alternatives open is infinite, limited only by the ingenuity of the analyst. The minimum aggregate costs of friction hypothesis will be correct only if no alternative to the free-market and perfect-knowledge assumptions results in lesser costs of friction. A few of these alternatives will be examined in the remainder of this section.

Consider first the existence of imperfect knowledge. Assume everybody has perfect knowledge, except for one individual. His landlord, taking advantage of the situation, charges him a rent greater than that the individual would pay if he were fully aware of all alternatives. In such a case, aggregate rents (and costs of friction) would exceed those resulting from the perfect-knowledge assumption by the excess in rent the landlord has been able to extract. But consider now the case in which everyone has perfect knowledge except for one landlord, who does not derive as high a price as he might for his land. In this case aggregate rents and costs of friction would be lower than under the perfect-knowledge assumption. Therefore, the relaxation of the assumption of perfect knowledge does not lead unequivocally to higher costs of friction, though in reality landlords tend to be the better informed, probably leading to higher rents.

Consider next the effect of zoning restrictions upon lot size. The usual type of zoning regulations set a minimum lot size in a section of the city. If the operation of the free market results in lots larger than this legal minimum in that area, then the restriction is not binding and is irrelevant for our purposes. However, if the restriction prescribes larger lots than would result from the operation of the free market, the price of land in that area will be lower under zoning restrictions than under the free market. This follows from the fact that the high bid in the free market situation is ruled out by the zoning ordinance, and the land is sold to lower bidders who comply with the lot-size requirements. Since density is lowered (that is, lot-size is increased) in this area by the zoning regulations, the result in the rest of the city is to lower supply relative to demand, increasing prices and densities. In short, prices are reduced in the zoned area and increased elsewhere and, according to the price elasticity of demand, the aggregate costs of friction may be increased or reduced.

Zoning regulations that set maximum lot sizes, where binding, would unequivocally reduce the costs of friction. Maximum-lot zoning would by definition reduce the amount of land bought. Prices would also be lowered because, density having increased, the size of the city would be smaller, and the bid price curves would run less distance from marginal to equilibrium price-locations (that is, less location differential rent). Since the city would have less spatial extension, transport costs would be less. Both components of the costs of friction, rent and transport, would be thus reduced. (See section D in this chapter for a fuller discussion of the effects of zoning.)

Consider lastly a case in which adjustment to changed conditions is not instantaneous. Suppose that X is the high bidder for a site at a certain location, but that he finds that the site is pre-empted by another tenant, Y, who holds a long-term lease. The rent paid by Y for that site is less than that which X would be willing to pay. X must now be satisfied with some other site. Suppose he decided on a more central and expensive location. This would reduce his transport costs. His rent (price times quantity) may be greater or less than he would pay at Y's location, for, though the price he must now pay is greater, he may maximize his revenue or satisfaction with a smaller site. If X decided on a less central location, his transport costs would increase and his rent payments might increase or decrease depending on the size of his lot. If in either case X's rent payments plus transport costs are greater than they would be if he had secured the location occupied by Y, aggregate costs of friction would increase only if the increase of the costs of friction of X exceed the savings that accrue to Y under the terms of his lease. Consequently, it is not clear whether the aggregate costs of friction would increase or decrease.

To summarize, the minimum aggregate costs of friction hypothesis is not valid when it is interpreted strictly in economic terms. When it is stated so that the costs of friction include disutility, it is undefinable and untestable. There is, moreover, a fundamental objection to its use as a guide for urban planning. The logic that would have the minimizing of the costs of friction be a planning objective is faulty in the same way that Haig's view of the location of the urban firm is faulty. The minimizing of a certain type of costs would be a valid approach only if all other costs and revenues (economic and psychological) remain constant. For instance, in the extreme case, a city could minimize its costs of friction by crowding all residences as tightly about the center of the city as is physically possible, and by forbidding all commercial and industrial development, thus reducing to zero the costs of friction of this sector. Such a solution would be, of course, absurd.

C. Income, Population Growth, and Technical Change

The model of the urban land market which was presented in the preceding chapters is a static model. That is to say, it does not, of itself, describe changes over time. However, certain inferences can be drawn about changes of the market as a whole by examining the effects of increases in income and population and changes of technology upon the bid price curves of the individual user. If a certain change affects all bid price curves in the same manner, the direction of its effect upon the market as a whole may be predicted.

The Effects of Income on Locations and Densities

In large American cities the higher-income residents locate farther away from the center of the city than those of lower incomes.[6] The principal explanation offered has been that, as the city grows, the wealthier build their houses on the vacant land on the periphery, leaving their old houses near the center to the poorer. This explanation is based on the growth of the city's population.[7] However, it can be shown that in a city which does not grow (that is, one corresponding to our static model), the same pattern of peripheral rich and central poor obtains, given certain tastes.

Let us examine the bid price curve of a resident. In chapter 4 we found that the marginal rate of substitution between land and the composite good is equal to the ratio of their prices.

$$(4:8) \qquad u_q/u_z = p_i(t)/p_z.$$

We also found that the marginal rate of substitution between movement from the center is equal to the ratio of their marginal costs:

$$(4:9) \qquad u_t/u_z = [q \, dp_i(t)/dt + dk/dt]/p_z.$$

Combining these equations, we obtain that the marginal rate of substitution between land and movement is equal to the ratio of their marginal costs:

$$(6:1) \qquad u_t/u_q = [q \, dp_i(t)/dt + dk/dt]/p_i(t).$$

To examine the slope of the bid price curve more easily, let us rewrite equation (6:1) as

$$(6:2) \qquad \frac{dp_i(t)}{dt} = \frac{p_i(t)}{q} \frac{u_t}{u_q} - \frac{1}{q} \frac{dk}{dt}.$$

6. This distribution by income has been established in a great many studies. One of the earliest statements occurs in the Park-Burgess concentric-zone hypothesis (*The City*).

7. See chapter 1, section C for a quotation from Hawley summarizing this explanatory theory and for comments on its dependence upon time and population growth.

It will be remembered from chapter 5 that the users of land with steeper curves will locate nearer the center of the city. Therefore, if we can show that higher incomes lead to more gently sloped curves, we may conclude that the wealthy will tend toward peripheral and the poorer toward central locations. To this purpose we shall examine the right side of equation (6:2), to see how the steepness of the bid price curve is affected by income for individuals of identical tastes. Three things will vary on the right side of equation (6:2) as income increases:[8]

(1) q increases with income, since it has a positive marginal utility. Since q is in the denominator of both terms of the right side of equation (6:2), this will lead to decreasing steepness with increasing income.[9]

(2) The marginal rate of substitution, u_t/u_q, may vary with income as the holdings of land increase. Normally, one would expect the marginal rate of substitution (which is here negative) to decrease with increasing income, for the marginal utility of land (u_q) will decrease as more land is held, whereas the marginal disutility of distance (u_t) may become more accented as accessibility becomes scarcer relative to land. This will lead to steeper curves with rising income. This factor will be examined further below.

(3) If commuting costs do not vary with income, the value of $-(1/q)dk/dt$ will increase with income because of the increasing q. This factor points unambiguously to a gentler slope and a peripheral location with increasing income.

Of the three elements, then, two (greater sensitivity to price changes and decreasing importance of commuting costs as a result of larger land holdings) point to a gentler slope and peripheral location with increasing income, and one (taste) points to a steeper slope and central location. Therefore, the net effect cannot be generalized. However, the alternatives may be more readily understood from a restatement of the conditions.

According to the term $-(1/q)dk/dt$, when land holdings are large

8. For the purpose of the analysis, the curves must be compared at a given price-location; consequently, distance and price are constant.

9. This effect has been noted by Arthur Row and Ernest Jurkat, "The Economic Forces Shaping Land Use Patterns," *J. Amer. Inst. of Planners*, 25:2 (May 1959).

a smaller rate of change in price is necessary to produce the income-effect to offset the increased commuting costs. For instance, a man holding one acre needs only a decrease in price of one dollar to offset an increase of one dollar in commuting costs. A man holding one tenth of an acre needs a decrease of ten dollars in price as compensation.

The term $[p_t(t)/q](u_t/u_q)$ is more complicated. Again, extensive land holdings militate for a gentler slope with rising income through q in the denominator. However, these very increases lead to a decrease of the negative term u_t/u_q, for accessibility may be expected to become more desirable as it becomes scarcer relative to land. If the marginal rate of substitution decreases at a faster rate than the holdings of land increase (that is, if there is no great desire to increase the quantity of land), the net result will be steeper bid price curves and a central location for the wealthy. However, if the desire for land is strong and not easily satisfied, the rate of decrease of the marginal rate of substitution will be less than the rate of increase of land, resulting in a gentler slope for a higher income.[10]

Some confirmation of the validity of these views can be obtained from the literature of human ecology. The American case, where the peripheral, suburban locations are occupied by the well-to-do, corresponds to the case of a slowly decreasing marginal rate of substitution.[11] In the preindustrial town, where there was slight differentiation in the size of lots, "the leading tradesmen live in the centre of town, the common people on the periphery."[12] Similar

10. Taking the extreme case, where the consumer does not care about accessibility or does not mind the bother of commuting ($u_t = 0$), the whole term $[p_t(t)/q]u_t/u_q$ will be zero, and the slope of the bid price curve will be determined by the amount of land and the marginal commuting costs in the term $-(1/q)dk/dt$, so that higher incomes will have gentler slopes. (This is the case considered by Beckman, in "On the Distribution of Rent and Residential Density in Cities.") However, the tendency toward gentler slopes for higher incomes will be even stronger where the marginal rate of substitution is a constant other than zero, for then the increasing q would add its effect on this constant to its effect on commuting costs.

11. The centrally located luxury apartments correspond to a minority of the wealthy, who strongly object to commuting and do not want a particularly spacious site. This corresponds to a rapidly decreasing marginal rate of substitution, and consequently steep bid price curves.

12. Gregor Paulson, *The Study of Cities* (Copenhagen: Munskgaard, 1959), p. 18. In ancient Athens "Demosthenes praised the leading men ... because they were satisfied with the same residences as other citizens" (p. 33). The location of the leading men was probably central.

conditions obtain in other cities of the world today in countries such as India and those of Latin America,[13] while some of the larger cities present a mixture of this pattern with the American.[14]

If this interpretation is correct, the peripheral location of the wealthy in American cities may be explained without referring to the growth of cities, and will not be limited to rapidly growing cities. The explanation of the spatial distribution which has just been put forth may be summarized in other terms. Given a strong appetite for land, so that the holdings of land vary greatly with income, the wealthier are affected relatively less by the costs of commuting because they spread these costs over larger sites. Consequently, the rich are price-oriented whereas the poor are location-oriented. Less accessibility being bought with increasing income, accessibility behaves as an inferior good. This is a possible explanation of the paradox encountered in American cities, of the poor living on expensive central land and the rich on cheaper peripheral land.

This is a point of some importance. If the peripheral location of the rich is due to increases in population and to the aging and obsolescence of more central housing, a governmental program of central redevelopment which provides downtown luxury apartments would lead, after some time, to centrally located rich and lower income people in the periphery, in the then aged suburban housing. If the view presented here is correct, and tastes do not change, the centrally located luxury apartments will satisfy only the limited demand of the rich with rapidly decreasing marginal rates of substitution and steep bid price curves, and the pattern of central poor and peripheral rich will prove lasting. Needless to say, the current boom in downtown construction of high-rent apartments on renewal sites will soon die as vacancies increase.

Population Growth

It is obvious that increases in population will result in higher land prices through an increase in the demand for land. The

13. See Theodore Caplow, "The Social Ecology of Guatemala City," *Social Forces*, 28:113–133 (Dec. 1949); and Noel P. Gist, "The Ecology of Bangalore, India: an East-West Comparison," *Social Forces*, 35:356–365 (May 1957).

14. See A. Bopegamage, *Delhi: A Study in Urban Sociology* (Bombay: University of Bombay Press, 1957). However, the large cities of developing countries present the phenomenon of squatters' colonies in the outskirts, arising from the rapid migration from the country to the city. These groups are largely unassimilated by the city, and are not accounted for in the model.

mechanics of the increase may be visualized by considering a distinct increase rather than a flow of immigration. The new occupants will each consume some land, so that the marginal location of the residential sector will move farther out from the center. Since the equilibrium bid price curves of the new residents must be fitted within the chain of marginal and equilibrium price-locations which constitute the price structure, each of the original occupants will have to shift to a higher bid price curve for his equilibrium. As a result of the higher prices, they will consume slightly less land than they did originally,[15] so that the net increase in the area of settlement will be less than the area occupied by the new population. Thus, other things being equal, an increase in population will result in higher prices and densities.[16]

It should be noted that, all other things being equal, with the poor in the center and the rich in the periphery, sheer population growth will push back the boundary between the rich and the poor, including some of the houses that were rich into the poor area. This phenomenon is quite ancient, as noted in a 1593 act of Parliament: "Great mischiefs daily grow and increase by reason of pestering the houses with diverse families, harboring of inmates, and converting great houses into several tenements, and exacting the erecting of new buildings in London and Westminster."[17] However, this process should not be confused with suburbanization, since over-all density is increasing rather than decreasing.

15. Louis Winnick notes that city size bears no relation to the persons-per-room ratio (*American Housing and Its Use: The Demand for Shelter Space* [New York: J. Wiley & Sons, 1957], pp. 65–66). This, however, does not disprove the theory: (1) income varies with size of city, affecting density; and (2) we are talking of persons-per-acre; the number of rooms is not predicted here, and is an intermediate variable obscuring the pattern. If we focus on a more homogeneous group, it has been noted that the size of the single-family-dwelling lot decreases with increasing population (Harland Bartholomew, *Urban Land Uses* [Cambridge, Mass.: Harvard University Press, 1932]).

16. If the price elasticity of demand were very great, prices and the area of settlement would increase very slightly, while density would increase sharply. Wingo, in *Transportation and Urban Land*, notes that it is possible, if the transportation system of a city is operating at full capacity, that a small increase in population will increase congestion greatly, making commuting more difficult and more expensive. The net effect might be a slight reduction of the area of the city. This would be equivalent to a negative technical change. See Technical Improvements in Transportation in this chapter.

17. Quoted by Lewis Mumford, *The Culture of Cities* (New York: Harcourt, Brace & Co., 1938), p. 123.

Technical Improvements in Transportation

Technical improvements in transportation may have two effects: (1) they may make commuting easier, and (2) they may make it less expensive. Both of these effects tend to reduce the steepness of the slope of residential bid price curves. It can be seen in equation (6:2) that making commuting easier reduces the marginal disutility of distance u_t (that is, it reduces the absolute value of the negative quantity u_t), resulting in a gentler slope. A reduction in the costs of commuting, on the other hand, would be reflected in a reduction of the term dk/dt, also resulting in a more gently sloped bid price curve. It is important to differentiate these two effects because various innovations may affect them differently. The automobile may be more expensive than public transportation (leading to steeper curves through increases in dk/dt), but may be a more pleasant way of commuting (leading to less steeply sloped curves through a decreased absolute value of u_t). Increases of population, though not in themselves a technical change, may lead to a situation where the city may enjoy the economies of scale of mass transportation. Then the cost may be reduced, but the associated congestion may make commuting more unpleasant.[18] In general, however, it is reasonable to expect that technical innovations will be accepted only when their net effect on cost and convenience is favorable. This will be reflected in more gently sloped bid price curves.[19]

What will be the effect of less steeply sloped bid price curves on the price structure? Will it be raised or lowered? The answer is that prices will be lower at the center and higher at the periphery. Examine Figure 32. The curve AB represents the price structure before the improvement of transportation. If there is no change in the size of lots, the chain of marginal and equilibrium price-locations

18. See Wingo, in *Transportation and Urban Land*, for the association of population growth and congestion or trip delays.

19. Improvements in the technology of transportation will result in more gently sloped bid price curves also for agriculture and the urban firm. In the case of agriculture, since rent is a residual after production and transportation costs, technical improvements that reduce the latter will reduce location differential rents. In the case of the urban firm, improvements in transportation will lead to smaller increases of operating costs with distance and greater acceptance by customers of stores in less accessible locations, so that sales volume will decrease less rapidly with increasing distance from the center. From equation (3:14) in chapter 3, this results in gentler bid price curves for urban firms.

resulting from more gently sloped bid price curves will be a curve such as $A'B$. However, since the prices of land in price structure $A'B$ are lower than the prices of curve AB, more land would be bought by the various users. The price structure that would result from the improvement of transportation would be a curve such as $A''B''$, where the additional acquisitions of land have pushed the marginal price-location from B to B''.[20]

It will be noted that the new equilibrium price structure, $A''B''$, assigns lower prices at central locations than did the original price structure, AB. However, the reader may be puzzled by the fact that

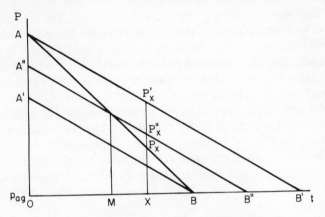

FIGURE 32. Effect of an improvement of transportation on the price structure

the price of land at distances greater than OM are greater after the improvement of transportation. The matter can be easily understood. Assume there is an individual whose equilibrium bid price curve before the technical change exactly coincides with the price structure AB.[21] After the technical improvement, his bid price curve AB' would represent the same level of satisfaction as curve

20. The curve $A''B''$, while higher than $A'B$, will not be as high as AB', for then, prices being everywhere higher than in the original price structure AB, the demand for land would be satisfied within some distance OX, smaller than OB. In such a case, the marginal price-location X would be inconsistent with the opportunity costs at that location.

21. The equilibrium location of such an individual would be indeterminate, but this does not affect the argument.

AB before it. That is to say, the individual would derive the same satisfaction from locating at X at price P'_x after the improvement as he would have at the lower price P_x before the improvement. He could derive the same level of satisfaction at a higher price because the technical improvement has reduced either or both the cost and the bother of commuting. Given a technical improvement, then, price P''_x at that location would represent a higher level of satisfaction than the lower P_x before the improvement. Thus, if we view the price structure as a generalized bid price curve, technical improvements could raise the price of land at the same time as satisfaction.

According to Haig, "an improvement in transportation, *ceteris paribus* will mean a reduction in friction and the diminution of the aggregate sum of site rentals."[22] However, this will be unequivocally true only if the *ceteris paribus* stricture applies to the size of the lot (yielding curve $A'B$ in Figure 32). Once we allow for the additional acquisition of land (curve $A''B''$), whether or not aggregate rents would be increased or diminished[23] would depend on the net effect of the price elasticities of the various consumers.

Economic Development: An Observation on Land Values in American Cities since World War II

Land values in American cities have boomed since World War II. Curiously, this boom has taken place largely in the periphery of metropolitan areas, while in the center land values have increased little and in some cases actually declined.[24] This contradicts ecological theory. R. Park, writing in 1929, theorized that improvements in transportation and population growth increased the advantage of the center.[25] Since World War II there has been a rapid increase in urban population, in automobile ownership, and

22. Haig, *Quarterly Journal of Economics*, 40:422. Ratcliff also endorses this view (*Urban Land Economics*, p. 372).

23. OAB (rotated $360°$) $\gtreqless OA''B''$ (rotated $360°$).

24. See, for instance, F. Fogarty, "Land: a New Kind of Boom," *Architectual Forum* (February and March 1957). McKenzie observed the same phenomenon in Chicago for the years 1921–1930 (*The Metropolitan Community*, p. 239).

25. Robert E. Park, *Human Communities* (Glencoe: The Free Press, 1952), p. 190. However, Park's argument was partly based on the inclusion of previously independent populations within the service area of the center.

in income. Why, then, has there not been a rise in land values at the center?

The answer to this question has been given in the preceding pages of this section, and it is only necessary to apply the conclusions. Let us examine the effects of the three changes we have selected: (1) increased automobile ownership and road improvements, (2) increased income per capita, and (3) increases in population.

It was shown above that, all other things being equal, improvements in transportation lead to higher peripheral and lower central prices. Thus, part of the observed changes in land prices since the war may be attributable to increased automobile ownership and improved road facilities.[26]

Similarly, we showed above, that—given our interpretation of American tastes—the richer tend to have more gently sloped bid price curves than the poorer. Since the war, personal income has risen, so that *everyone's* curves are less steeply sloped. While in this case we cannot set an upper limit to the new price structure as we did for transportation improvements, a more gently sloped price structure means that the relative increase in prices at the periphery will be greater than at the center, where they may even decrease. Thus, increases in income per capita may also serve to explain the differences in the increases of central and peripheral land prices.

Population growth leads to increased land prices at the center as well as at the periphery. But, all other things being equal, an increase in population will lead to a higher price structure very similar in shape to the original one. Examine Figure 33. At the center, prices rise from OA to OA', while at a peripheral location such as t_x they will rise from P_x to P'_x, both changes being nearly equal in absolute terms. At the peripheral location, where the original price was lower, the percentage increase will be much greater than at the center.

The explanation just presented has taken into account only three factors. Though there are undoubtedly others, these have been chosen as typical of periods of rapid economic development, which are characterized and even defined by population growth and urbanization, technical change, and increasing income per capita.

26. These improvements may be counterbalanced by increased congestion, but the net effect is presumably favorable.

The suburbanization of metropolitan areas is a phenomenon related to that of the different rates of growth of central and peripheral land values. Suburbanization refers not only to the increase in size of an urban area, so that it exceeds its original municipal boundaries, but also to a change in kind, to the lower densities characteristic of the suburbs.[27] The suburbanization of metropolitan areas has often been explained by the rapid growth of metropolitan populations. However, the foregoing analysis makes clear that population growth without increased income per capita

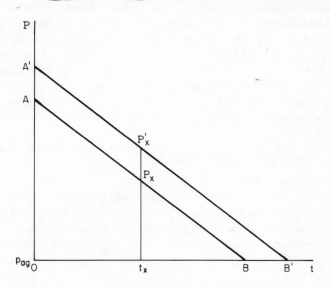

FIGURE 33. Effect of population growth on the price structure

or improved transportation would lead to some increase in size of the city, but would have the effect opposite to suburbanization of increasing densities, through the increase of demand without a corresponding increase of supply. An increase in per capita income or an improvement in transportation without population growth, on the other hand, would lead not only to an increase in size of the urban area but also to suburbanization in the sense of lower

27. See, for instance, Amos Hawley, *The Changing Shape of Metropolitan America: Deconcentration since 1920* (Glencoe: The Free Press, 1956), p. 13ff.

densities. Thus, metropolitan areas with improving transportation and increasing income may be expected to suburbanize more rapidly in the sense of a low-density suburban type of settlement in the absence of population growth. Population growth militates against suburbanization in this sense.

The phenomenon of suburbanization, needless to say, is not unique to the postwar period. It has been proceeding during all of the twentieth century, and it had begun, for the same reasons, in the nineteenth century. Population growth, the effect of income, and transportation improvements are implicit when Tunnard says, "American and English cities were suburbanizing themselves at about the same time the nineteenth century . . . The precedent was set by the rich, or by the fashionable intellectuals . . . Produced by an expanded mercantilism, these suburbs were within easy reach of town by carriage, coach, or waterway."[28] One may note too that the great real estate fortunes, such as the Astor's, were made in speculation on suburban, rather than central land.

The Effects of Taxation on Land

A tax on land in the form of a percentage of rents collected will be borne by the landlords and will not affect land prices or the pattern of settlement. Examine Figure 27 in chapter 5. If any portion of the rents are taken through taxation, the pattern will remain the most profitable for the landlord and the most satisfactory for the tenants. In this the theory arrives at the conclusion of traditional theory of rent.

A flat-rate tax, on the other hand, will be borne by the tenants if it is levied only upon occupied land. Its effect is to make greater than zero the price of land at the margin of the economy. The chain of marginal and equilibrium price-locations would become correspondingly higher. But if the tax is levied on all land, whether or not occupied, it will be borne by the landlord. At the marginal location of the economy, any price, however small (that is, zero) will help the landlord to carry the burden of taxation, and the chain of marginal and equilibrium price-locations will be the same as if there were no tax.

28. Christopher Tunnard, *The City of Man* (New York: Chas. Scribner's Sons, 1953), p. 180.

D. Zoning

Either the type of land use or the density or intensity of land use may be zoned. Zoning is, of course, a legal statement of what use of the land will or will not be acceptable to a governmental authority, and therefore represents a potential modification of the free-market situation. It will not always be a modification since usually zoning regulations and the free-market result coincide, so that the regulations do not bind. In fact, zoning boards often follow, though sometimes reluctantly, the dictates of the market, and even try to anticipate them, both in framing the regulations and in granting exemptions and variances. The view is often expressed, as in the case of "large-lot" zoning, that the zoning authority is opposing the market forces in the short run only to serve them more perfectly in the long run, by holding land to "maturity" before allowing it to be developed. But rather than discuss these institutional aspects of zoning, we shall only consider its effects, when it binds, upon price, density, occupancy, et cetera, in terms of the general theory being presented. When it does not bind, it will not affect the free-market solution.

Land Use Zoning

Land use zoning states that certain land may not be put to certain uses. This type of regulation binds, of course, only when the proscribed land use would use that land if the market were free; that is to say, when the proscribed land use would make the highest bid. The bid price function of that land use may be viewed as discontinuous over the land it may not occupy. The next highest bid allowed by the zoning regulations will take the land. In operating the model, therefore, all that is necessary is to specify the discontinuity of certain bid price functions over certain areas of land, and to form the chain of equilibrium and marginal price-locations in the light of this.

The effects of a binding land use zoning regulation are simple. On the site directly affected, since the highest bid is disallowed, a lower bid takes precedence, and the price of land on that site will be lower than under free-market conditions. For the zoned-out land use, since its free-market equilibrium bid price function is not permitted, it will be forced to a higher one, resulting in lower profits or utility, or in a higher price of agricultural product, depending on the type of land use. In less exact terms, this may be viewed as the result of a reduction in the supply of land available to that land use. For the other land uses, on the other hand, such zoning means a slight reduction in the competing demand and a slight increase in the supply of land, permitting them slightly lower equilibrium bid price curves.

An interesting speculation concerns a city which, having had a free land market, one day passes a comprehensive, exclusive land use zoning ordinance, so that every piece of land can be occupied only by the type of land use currently occupying it. This, of course, would create as many discrete, independent land markets as categories of land use, in place of the single, free market, in which all land uses are interdependent. At first sight, it might seem that each of the discrete land markets will have a marginal price of zero, and that the chain of marginal and equilibrium price-locations will rise only to a modest height in each market, the over-all price structure resulting being like the tooth edge of a saw. If this were true, total rents would be very much lower, and since every one would be on a lower bid price curve, the satisfaction of residents and the profits of business would be higher, and agricultural prices would be lower. This, however, only illustrates the dangers of the neglect of quantities. Since prices are lower, price elasticity for land being positive, occupants would prefer larger sites. Taking advantage of this, landlords could raise the price of land: if the current occupant will not pay, his neighbors in the same type of land use will take over his land since their quantity-demand is unsatisfied. Landlords can continue to raise the price until there is no more unmet demand for lot-size expansion. This will lead to a level of prices such that all the land is taken, and every occupant has as much land as he wants at that price. This, of course, is exactly the original price structure under the free market. The type of follow-the-leader zoning we have been considering would not be binding and would not affect the regional structure.

Density-intensity zoning

This type of zoning sets limits to the rate of occupancy of land. In the usual case, it sets a maximum rate of occupancy by setting a minimum lot-size per family in residential land uses, but for completeness we shall also consider zoning that sets minimum rates of occupancy by setting maximum lot-size per family. The usual regulation may say, for instance, that houses for not more than two families may be built on a lot 60' × 80', thus setting a maximum rate of occupancy of one family per 2,400 square feet. A zoning regulation might set a minimum rate of occupancy by permitting no house a site larger than a certain size.

Density zoning may best be understood by examining further the nature of the bid price function. We have considered the bid price of a resident as being a function of distance, $p(t)$, with the quantity of land optimized at every point. But we must consider now bid price for quantities other than the optimal, so that we are in fact dealing with a function of distance and quantity, $p(t, q)$. It can be shown that at any given distance, bid price will be at a maximum at the equilibrium quantity of land, and that lower prices will be bid if the zoning regulations force the occupant to buy more or less land than he wants. Thus, if the zoning regulations compel the resident to buy more land than he would under the free-market conditions, the resident will bid less per unit of land. If, on the other hand, there is maximum-lot zoning they do not permit him to have as much land as he would like. To maintain the constant satisfaction of the bid price curve, he will have to make up the foregone land by purchases of the composite good exceeding in value that of the lack of land.[29]

A bid price function of price with quantity is shown on Figure 34, where q_e is the equilibrium quantity of land that would be bought under free-market conditions at price p_e. To the left of q_e the bid price function shows the prices that would be bid at the same level

---

29. The exact proof follows. Consider the utility and budget equations: (4:6) $u_0 = u(t, q, z)$; (4:7) $y = p_z z + p_i(t, q)q + k(t)$. Note that the bid price, p_i, is now a function of quantity as well as distance. From the conditions of maximum satisfaction, in a manner parallel to the derivation of equation (4:9) we obtain for any given t, $u_q/u_z = [q\, dp_i/dq + p_i(q)]/p_z$, which may be rewritten as $dp_i/dq = [(u_q/u_z)p_z - p_i(q)]/q$. When q is at the equilibrium position that would obtain under free-market conditions, equation (4:8) states that $u_q/u_z = p_i/p_z$, so that $dp_i/dq = 0$. When q, through maximum-lot zoning, is smaller than the free-market equilibrium quantity, $u_q/u_z > p_i/p_z$, and the bid price curve will be sloped positively with quantity ($dp_i/dq > 0$). When q, through minimum-lot zoning, is larger than it would be under free-market conditions, $u_q/u_z < p_i/p_z$, and the bid price curve will slope downward with quantity ($dp_i/dq < 0$). In other words, the free-market equilibrium value of q corresponds to the maximum bid price at a given level of satisfaction, and bid prices will be lower for all other values of q.

of satisfaction under binding maximum-lot regulations, and to the right of q_e, the bid prices for binding minimum-lot regulations.

By referring now to Figure 35, we may study the effects of residential lot-size zoning. Diagrams A and B consider the two basic cases of zoning that sets a minimum lot-size. Diagrams C and D consider the two basic cases of zoning that sets a maximum lot-size. The vertical lines at the a, b, b', and c values on the q-axis indicate four alternative minimum or maximum lot-sizes. In the case of the

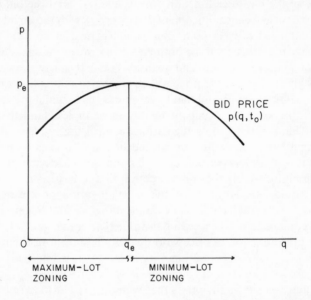

FIGURE 34. Bid price as a function of quantity at a given location

minimum lot-size, any lot larger than that specified in the regulations is permissible, while in the case of maximum lot-size any smaller lot is permitted. To assist in reading the diagram, small arrows pointing to the right in A and B and to the left in C and D have been added. Diagrams A and C consider the case in which the higher free-market bid (p_y) would be made for a small lot (q_y), and diagrams B and D the case in which the higher free-market bid (p_Y) is made for a larger lot (q_Y). Since, given similar tastes, rich people will buy more land, the bid price function of quantity which reaches its apex at the greater quantity of land may be presumed to belong to a wealthier individual. To indicate this, the curves have been labeled bp_y and bp_Y, where Y is the richer. Their respective free-market equilibrium quantities of land are q_y and q_Y, and their bid prices for these quantities p_y and p_Y.

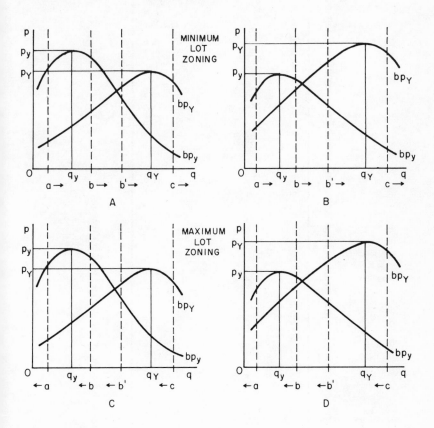

FIGURE 35. Effects of maximum- and minimum-lot zoning (see Table 3)

In Table 3 are set out the occupants, quantities, and prices arising in every case of Figure 35, as well as those that would result under free-market conditions.

TABLE 3. Occupancy, size of lot, and price of land according to the free-market and various zoning conditions

| | Minimum-lot zoning | | | | | | Maximum-lot zoning | | | | | |
| | Diagram A | | | Diagram B | | | Diagram C | | | Diagram D | | |
Conditions	Occupant	Quantity	Price	Occupant	Quantity	Price	Occupant	Quantity	Price	Occupant	Quantity	Price
Free market	y	q_y	p_y	Y	q_Y	p_Y	y	q_y	p_y	Y	q_Y	p_y
Case a	y	q_y	p_y	Y	q_Y	p_Y	y	a	$<p_y$	$y*$	a	$<p_y$
Case b	y	b	$\left\{\begin{array}{l}<p_y\\ >p_y\end{array}\right.$	Y	q_Y	p_Y	y	q_y	p_y	$y*$	q_y	p_y
Case b'	$Y*$	q_Y	p_Y	Y	q_Y	p_Y	y	q_y	p_y	Y	b'	$\left\{\begin{array}{l}>p_y\\ <p_y\end{array}\right.$
Case c	$Y*$	c	$<p_Y$	Y	c	$<p_Y$	y	q_y	p_y	Y	q_Y	p_Y

NOTE: See Figure 35

* Indicates a change in occupant from the free-market situation.

In Diagram A, under free-market conditions, the land would go to the lower-income individual, who would buy q_y at p_y. If the minimum lot is set at a, the zoning regulation is not binding, and there is no change. If it is set at b, the lower-income individual still makes the high bid, but one lower than p_y, since he is being forced to buy more land than he wants. When the minimum lot-size reaches some level b', the bid of the lower-income person drops below the level of p_Y, and the land will pass to the higher-income person who will enjoy his equilibrium quantity q_Y at his equilibrium price p_Y. Further increases in the minimum lot-size will not affect the occupancy by the higher-income person, though after it reaches values greater than q_Y (such as c), the bid price will drop below p_Y.

In Diagram B, under free-market conditions, the land would go to the richer individual, who bids price p_Y for q_Y land. Minimum-lot zoning will not be binding until it reaches a level higher than q_Y (such as c), when the price will drop below p_Y, without a change in occupant.

Diagram C considers the effects of maximum-lot zoning, which is in practice very rarely used. In this case, under free-market conditions, the lower-income person makes the high bid p_y for quantity q_y of land. If the maximum lot is set at a, the land will still be occupied by the lower-income person, though he will pay a price lower than p_y since he does not get as much land as he wants. Minima higher than q_y would not affect the free-market resolution.

Diagram D also considers maximum-lot zoning, but in this case the higher-income person makes the high free-market bid: p_Y for q_Y land. Setting the maximum lot at a would change occupancy to the lower-income person, but he would pay a price lower than p_y since he does not get as much land as he would like. If the maximum lot-size is set at b, the lower-income person would still take the land, and he would settle on his own free-market equilibrium position, buying q_y land at p_y. However, when the maximum lot-size reaches b', the bid price of the high-income bidder will exceed p_y, though he does not get as much land as he wants, and therefore occupancy will revert to the higher-income person, who would buy b' land. Finally, when maximum lot-size exceeds q_Y, as in the case of c, the zoning regulation is not binding.

Operation of the Model

The model suggested in chapter 5 for the free market may still be used, but with the restriction that in areas where the zoning regulation is binding upon some bid price functions, these be calculated over these areas not by permitting q to vary to optimize satisfaction, but by fixing q at the zoned value for the curves that are bound. With this provision, bid price functions may be used to build up the chain of marginal and equilibrium price-locations. It will be noted from Table 3 that the quantity of land is in all cases either the free-market quantity or the zoned maximum or minimum, but never another value.

Zoning Policy and Urban Renewal

In section C of this chapter it was observed that, given the appetite for land which seems to predominate in American tastes, the rich will tend to peripheral locations and the poor to central locations. It was suggested that current urban renewal programs tend to assume implicitly that the substitution of high-rent apartments for slums in central locations will attract the rich, and that the lower-income groups will be able to occupy the then aging peripheral houses. Thus, the city would renew itself by flows of the rich toward the center and of the poor toward the edges, in a manner similar to the convection currents in a pot of boiling water. But our analysis of the location choices showed, if correct, that the rich will not be attracted to the center, while the poor prefer central locations.

The analysis of the effects of zoning, however, suggests a method by which these location choices may be changed. From our analysis of the effects of income and distance on bid price in section C, we concluded that the rich will make the higher bids in the periphery of the city, while the poor will make them near the center. We may then conclude that Diagrams B and D in Figure 35 would apply typically to peripheral locations, while Diagrams A and C would apply typically to central locations. By referring to Table 3, we may observe that the minimum-lot zoning in the peripheral location (B) leaves the land in the hands of the wealthy, while the maximum-lot zoning in the peripheral location (D) gives the land to the lower-income bidder when the maximum is set sufficiently low. Conversely, in the center of the city, minimum-lot zoning A can shift the occupancy from the lower- to the higher-income, while maximum-lot zoning C in all cases leaves the lower-income as the occupant.

This strongly suggests that a vigorous metropolitan zoning regulation is a necessary adjunct to current renewal practices. This zoning would set minimum-lot requirements in central locations, changing the occupancy to higher incomes, and maximum-lot regulations in peripheral locations, changing the occupancy to lower incomes. It must be observed that current zoning practice tends to defeat current renewal practice by setting high minimum-lot restrictions in peripheral locations. It must also be observed that, since metropolitan government is an obvious necessity for the comprehensive, coordinated zoning just suggested, the recognition of the interdependence of zoning and renewal activities constitutes a very strong argument for metropolitan government, at least with respect to these functions.

E. EMPIRICAL TESTING OF THE THEORY AND OPERATIONAL MODELS

What evidence is there that the theory presented in these pages is more than a lengthy formal exercise? There is, to be sure, the weight of opinion of many writers, who attribute considerable importance to land values as the basic distributing factor in the spatial structuring of the city. There is, too, whatever plausibility the theory may have. There is the evidence of regularities in the spatial structure of cities, gathered in many studies, which argues for some socioeconomic mechanism in which distance is an important element, as it is in our theory. But these are indirect evidence for the particular form of the theory here presented. In the next few pages a possible manner of testing the theory will be presented in broad outline.

In the enormous body of literature on the city there is much empirical evidence from which may be inferred a statistical association of income and distance with the price of land, but this writer does not know of any published work that precises this relationship. This is probably because, on the one hand, of the difficulty of obtaining data and, on the other, of the absence of any explicit theory. However, a theory based on these variables depends on the demonstration of such a relationship. Consequently, it was decided to test for the simple question: is the amount spent for land associated with income and with distance from the center of the city?

Data for Philadelphia for the years 1950–1952 were obtained and a regression with these variables was calculated. The number of observations is small and the data not altogether satisfactory, but a significant correlation was obtained.[30] The equation obtained is:

$$pq = -222.65 + 0.4357\,(\pm 0.1275)y - 90.107\,(\pm 22.703)t$$

$$R = 0.69 \qquad S = 375.67$$

term.

p: price per square foot, in dollars;
q: number of square feet per family;
y: family income, in dollars;
t: distance from the center of the city, in miles.

It will be noted that the signs of the independent variables are in the expected directions: expenditure increases with income and decreases with distance from the center. Thus, we have shown association among the variables,[31] and their effects upon each other are in the expected directions. The results justify a theory in terms of these variables, but, of course, they do not prove it.

The Philadelphia data show the usual regularities: (1) price decreases with distance from the center; (2) density decreases with distance from the center, or, in other words, lot-size increases with distance from the center; (3) site-size, q, increases with income; and (4) distance from the center increases with income.[32] An interesting question suggests itself: since density decreases and family income increases with distance from the center, what is the net result in terms of family income per acre? In other words, does "income-density" increase or decrease with distance from the center? The Philadelphia data show that at distances greater than 12 minutes from the center "income-density" decreases with increases in

30. Exact definitions of these variables as well as their sources are given in appendix C.

31. There is considerable intercorrelation among these and other variables, such as type and age of housing. Therefore, the validity of the selection of variables must be justified in terms of theory, since other variables may yield equally reliable regression equations.

32. The following regression was calculated for census tracts: $t = 1.88 + 0.488y$; $r = 0.84$; $S_y = 3.92$; $N = 62$; $\bar{t} = 17.51$, in minutes of travel to the center of the city, as calculated by the Philadelphia City Planning Commission; $\bar{y} = 32.06$ in hundreds of dollars, is median income per family, from the tracts statistics of the 1950 U.S. Census. A few tracts for which the P.C.P.C. gave alternative travel times were not included in the computation.

distance,[33] indicating that site-size, q, increases faster than income. Under the 12-minute distance, the situation is less clear. Several points lie near the extended regression line and within the standard error. But a large number of tracts lie under these limits. Almost all these tracts are of extremely low median family income; 13 out of 18 in the $700 to $1,500 range. Five of six tracts within one standard error are in the $1,900 to $2,700 range, and the three tracts above this are in the range between $2,000 and $2,900.

A clearer picture emerges when the "income-density" is plotted against median family income. The point distribution is like an inverted V, income per acre rising with median family income (at a rate of approximately $6,700 per acre per hundred dollars increase in family income), reaching an apex when family income is about $2,700 (some $400 under the median of tract incomes), and then decreasing (again, at a rate of $6,700 per acre per hundred dollars increase in family income).

These findings may be significant not only for studies in marketing[34] and taxation, but they also throw light on the income elasticity of the demand for land. It shows that the income elasticity (per cent change in site-size divided by per cent change in income) is greater than zero but less than one for low incomes (up to $2,700 per family), and greater than one thereafter.[35]

33. $y/q = 222 - 5.35t$; $r = -0.63$; $S_y = 37.0$; $N = 49$; $\overline{(y/q)} = 119.2$ in thousands of dollars is family income per net residential acre, calculated by the P.C.P.C.; $\overline{t} = 20.4$ is the traveling distance to the center of the city, in minutes. Within 3 standard deviations of Fisher's z-transformation, r might range from -0.283 to -0.828, so that while the correlation is not high, it is quite significant. In judging the correlation coefficient and the standard error it must be remembered that the data used contains large probable errors of measurement. The income figure is an estimate of mean income from median income information from the U.S. Census, made by the P.C.P.C., and the quality of the site-size data is discussed in appendix C. Since the dependent variable is a ratio of these two measurements, their errors are compounded. The independent variable is again time-distance, which usually contains many possibilities of error, and tracts were grouped within relatively gross categories within isochrones. In view of this, the relatively low coefficient of correlation was to be expected.

34. It will be recognized that income-density is the limiting case in population-income potential models (developed by the social physicists and now gaining favor with marketing, traffic, and other analysts) when the exponent of distance approaches infinity.

35. The change in income per acre is $\Delta(y/q) = (y_1/q_1) - (y_0/q_0)$. If we define $\Delta y = y_1 - y_0$ and $\Delta q = q_1 - q_0$, and substitute above for y_0, q_0, the equality reduces to $\Delta(y/q) = (\Delta y q_1 - q y_1)/q_1(q_1 - \Delta q)$, and the slope of the curve will be: $\Delta(y/q)/\Delta y = [q - (\Delta q/\Delta y)y]/q(q - \Delta q) = [1 - (\Delta q/q)(y/\Delta y)]/(q - \Delta q)$. It will be observed that the

It must be pointed out, however, that this income elasticity of land is a gross measure, since the change in the quantity of land is the result not only of changes in income, but also of the choice of location, which determines land price and commuting cost. Thus, this gross income elasticity is the combined result of net income elasticity (constant price and commuting costs), of price elasticity, and of the income effect of commuting costs.

Confirmation of the validity of our theory must await more ambitious empirical studies. A variety of tests is possible, from sociopsychological studies of tastes to detailed studies of expenditure patterns.[36] Here, however, a suggestion will be made of a possible test of the conclusions of the theory rather than of its roots and assumptions. One might try to find bid price curves for groups of like families. Families in such groups should be similar in income and tastes. Similarity of income, of course, can be obtained by subdividing the population of the city into income groups. Similarity of tastes is harder to establish. In general, however, tastes or preferences may be assumed to be more or less homogeneous within certain groups, defined by such characteristics as family size, occupation,[37] and race or ethnic origin.[38] The population of the city may be divided into a number of groups by such classifications. A regression of the observed price on distance for each of these groups should yield the equilibrium bid price curves of all groups.[39]

---

denominator must be positive, and that the expression $(\Delta q/q)(y/\Delta y)$ in the numerator is the income elasticity. Therefore the slope of income per acre plotted against income per family will be positive when income elasticity is less than one, and negative when it is greater than one. That the income elasticity, even at very low incomes, is greater than zero can be calculated from the data, thus justifying statistically the general assumption of a positive marginal utility of land.

36. For instance, it has been observed that the secular drop during the past half century in the portion of the consumer's dollar spent on housing has been almost exactly balanced by the increased expenditures in transportation and recreation. The same complementarity is observable in studies of the effects of economic cycles on consumer expenditures. See Nelson N. Foote, J. Abu-Lughod, M. M. Foley, and L. Winnick, *Housing Choices and Housing Constraints* (New York: McGraw-Hill, 1960).

37. For instance, it has been found that blue and white collar workers at the same income levels have different residential patterns, and, by inference, different tastes. See O. D. and B. Duncan, "Residential Distribution and Occupational Stratification," *The Amer. J. of Sociology*, 60:493–503 (Mar. 1955).

38. See, for instance, Leo Grebler, *Housing Market Behavior in a Declining Area* (New York: Columbia University Press, 1952).

39. While the division of the city's population according to tastes would be *ad hoc*,

Since the observations used to calculate these regressions would of necessity be of prices at locations actually occupied by the group, by definition they would apply only to the equilibrium bid price curves. However, a more complete bid price curve mapping might be obtained by calculating regression equations for the same groups in cities of different size and different population composition. Variations on the supply side might be considered as well by examining cities in which the quantities of land available at various distances differ. Finally, a complete mapping of bid price curves for each group might be obtained by interpolation. If at the same time regression equations are computed for size of lot (the inverse of net residential density) on distance, one would have the essentials of an operational predictive model.[40] Given a population prediction for some future date in terms of these groups, a market solution can be found by the method described in chapter 5. The solution would be indeterminate as to the location of individuals within groups, but the method would not be affected. Note that in this case no assumption is necessary as to the shape of individual lots. This solution would predict the extension and internal densities of the city,[41] as well as the price structure and the location of these groups.

The reader may feel that this prospect of empirical testing and predictive models is too sanguine. The statistical and definitional problems are certain to be difficult, and the data hard to obtain (in particular, land values).[42] Moreover, there can be no triumphal arrival at predictive models if the empirical tests discredit the theory. However, even should the theory be disproved, this would represent

---

the division into income classes should yield, according to the theory, significantly different regression coefficients between groups. On the other hand, the relevance of the subdivision of the population into groups using criteria such as family size and occupation would be confirmed according to whether or not the regression coefficients were significantly different among groups.

40. In homogenizing the data among cities, constraints upon the size of the lot should be taken into account. These constraints may be zoning regulations or the subdivision of the land into lots years before actual development takes place, as in Chicago. This may make it possible to get bid price as a function of both distance and land quantity, as in the analysis of zoning in section D of this chapter.

41. Wingo, in *Transportation and Urban Land*, remarks that, while the price structure will be a smooth function, densities may show sharp changes in the boundaries between groups.

42. See appendix C for a discussion of some of these problems and one way of handling them.

a clear advance in our knowledge, forcing the theories in human ecology and land economics to re-examine their basic tenets.

In regressions for bid price curves such as those just proposed, the error term would be of particular interest. Aside from error in measurement, the difference between the observed price of land and the regression value at a location may be attributed to variables which are not considered in the theory. Thus, while we assume a featureless plain, cities in reality are built on high and low ground, are traversed by rivers, and have certain prevailing winds. The difference between the actual price of land at a location and the value calculated from the bid price regression of the group which occupies that location may be interpreted as a measure of its attractiveness. Moreover, we have assumed "economic men," whereas in reality men are social animals as well. The deviance between observed and calculated values may serve to measure the relative social attractiveness of an area for the group that occupies it. For instance, we may find that the lower status white collar groups pay a higher price in areas occupied by higher status groups than for otherwise equivalent areas occupied by blue collar workers. The error term of the regression, then, may serve to measure quantitatively the effect of certain variables which are generally considered important but which elude direct measurement.

F. City Shapes

Thus far we have considered distance as a radial measurement from the center of the city. As a result, we have obtained a city patterned in concentric rings, very like the concentric-zone city of Park and Burgess.[43] However, this simple arrangement of rings is rapidly complicated by refinements in the concept of distance. The simplest of these consists of measuring distance from any point to the center along existing routes rather than simply measuring air distance. Points at the same travel distance from the center of the city may be connected by iso-access lines, as in Figure 36. Here a grid street pattern has been assumed. The center of the city is indicated by a large dot. The locus of a given travel distance will be a square

43. See Park and Burgess, *The City*. For a summary of this theory, see Chauncy D. Harris and E. L. Ullman, "The Nature of Cities," *The Annals*, 242:7–17 (Nov. 1945).

(rotated 45 degrees from the axes of the streets), containing an area equal to twice the square of the linear distance traveled. A problem involving such a street pattern could be solved by the method described in chapter 5. The equation for the availability of land would be $S(t) = 2t^2$, where t is now travel distance.[44] The resulting pattern of settlement would be one of concentric square rings rather than concentric circular rings.[45] Other street patterns would yield other patterns for the city. The city will remain essentially ring-shaped as long as the street pattern is radially symmetrical, but irregular street layouts will do away with annular zones to a greater or lesser extent. The logic and method of solution just presented are

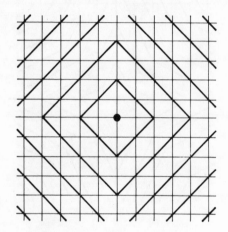

FIGURE 36. Isochrones on a uniform rectangular street grid

not affected if t is measured along existing roads rather than radially from the center, though the mechanics of obtaining the $S(t)$ equation become slightly more complicated.

44. If the street pattern is known, the area covered by streets should be deducted for greater accuracy. If streets are s feet wide and blocks b feet on the side, the deduction for streets would make the availability of land equation $S(t) = 2t^2 b^2/(b + s/2)^2$.

45. An approximation of this pattern can be seen in the land values of Chicago in the mid-nineteenth century. See Homer Hoyt, *One Hundred Years of Land Values in Chicago* (Chicago: University of Chicago Press, 1933), Fig. 11, p. 71 (year 1856), Fig. 12, p. 72 (year 1857), and Fig. 21, p. 114 (year 1873). Egon Bergel has suggested that the Park-Burgess theory be converted to a rectangular scheme, though he does not mention the 45-degree rotation (*Urban Sociology* [New York: McGraw-Hill, 1955], p. 109ff.).

A further refinement may be introduced into the measurement of distance by measuring travel along different types of roads in different types of units. Thus, a mile traveled by train or on a super-highway may be equivalent to one thousand feet traveled by street-car or on a crowded city street. In Figure 37 iso-access lines are shown schematically for a city having two highways, XX and YY, crossing at right angles at the center of the city. The rest of the city has a grid system of streets on which travel is h times harder than on the highways. If the center of the city is designated as the origin

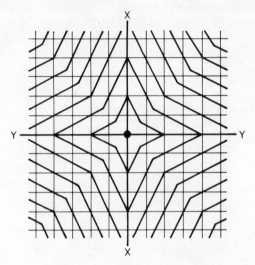

FIGURE 37. Isochrones on a rectangular street grid with two intersecting highways

$(0, 0)$, the minimum travel distance t of any point (x, y) is given by the equation

$$
\begin{cases}
t = \dfrac{|x|}{h} + |y| & \text{when } |x| > |y| \\[2ex]
t = |x| + \dfrac{|y|}{h} & \text{when } |x| < |y|
\end{cases}
$$

The iso-access lines in this case will form a four-point star. The availability of land equation $S(t)$ will be the integral of the function described by the iso-access lines, and it could be obtained for any given *t* by running a planimeter over the corresponding iso-access curve. More complex geometries, involving roads of different speeds that formed loops, rays, secants, et cetera, could be handled similarly.[46] In Figure 38 is shown a schematic drawing of the iso-access curves resulting from a square loop of high-speed highways and two highways intersecting at the center of the basic grid pattern.

FIGURE 38. Isochrones on a rectangular street grid with two intersecting highways and a rectangular loop

However, where different types of transportation are available (for example, roads of different quality, or public versus private

46. C. B. Hayes, in an interesting empirical study of land values along a railroad line, finds a general decrease in land values from the center of Chicago, but there is a ridge along the railroad line, with a prominent pyramid centered around each station. This conforms exactly with the theoretical approach being outlined. C. B. Hayes, "Suburban Residential Land Values along the C. B. & Q. Railroad," *Land Economics*, 33:177–181 (May 1957).

transportation), there results not only a complication of the geometry of the problem—which could be handled—but there also arises a conceptual problem. One often finds in the literature facile references to curves of equal time-cost of travel. Obviously, both the variables of time and cost are important to our theory (as are the variables of comfort, freedom, and convenience, and their opposite, disutility). The former is reflected in the utility function of the individual, the latter in the costs of commuting in his budget balance equation, and both in the equation relating marginal rate of substitution to marginal costs. The problem is that a highway may halve travel time but increase the cost of travel. In other words, time and cost vary independently to some extent, and since there are two types of units, distances on routes of different types cannot be compared directly. An index number might perhaps be found empirically by comparing price differentials along equal stretches of different types of roads, but its meaning would be unclear, and its value variable. It would be difficult but more satisfactory to measure both time and cost to each location, and to have bid price be a function of both these variables.[47]

The concept of the center of the city may be refined as well. Thus far we have assumed a single, all-purpose center,[48] but other forms may be considered. The simplest complication would be to consider two independent centers, *A* and *B* in Figure 39. Each center serves its own population. If the two centers are close enough that the population of both bids for some of the same land, that land will go to the highest bidder. The resulting pattern would be as in Figure 39. The upper part of the figure represents a map view. The boundary between the areas of occupancy of the populations of the two centers, if their rent surfaces are identical, will be a straight line *LL* normal to a line drawn between the two centers. The lower part of

47. The problem is further complicated by the possibility of alternative means of travel from one point to another. Perhaps this difficulty could be reduced by using the time and cost of the means principally used to travel for that particular trip. However, to do justice to the problem, a very elaborate theoretical analysis would be necessary, involving delicate substitutions between the time, the cost, and the comfort of travel. Cf. Wingo, *Transportation and Urban Land*, for the combination of time and cost.

48. Though not all employment, shopping, et cetera are at the center, this will be the point of greater accessibility to these activities. The center of the city is analogous to the center of gravity of a physical object.

the figure shows the prices paid for land, the dashed lines representing unsuccessful bids by the population on the other side of the boundary line *LL.* A similar situation is depicted for a large

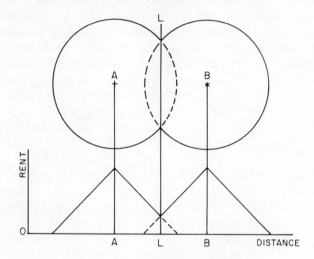

FIGURE 39. Rent patterns of two competing neighboring centers of the same size

metropolitan center *A* and a smaller center *B* in Figure 40. The population centered around *B* is completely surrounded by the population of *A.* The prices paid by the population of *B* are higher than they would be if *B* were an independent center, for the marginal prices are determined in competition with the population of *A.* The prices that would be paid if *B* were by itself on the plain would be at some lower level, schematically represented by the shaded area in the lower part of the figure, and the density of settlement would be lower.

The logic and the geometry when two or more centers are competing for the land is parallel in the urban and the agricultural cases.[49] However, in the urban case there may be several meanings to the words "competing centers." First, they may be competing

49. For an analysis of competing centers in the agricultural case, see E. S. Dunn, *The Location of Agricultural Production,* chap. 5, and C. D. and W. P. Hyson, "The Economic Law of Market Areas," *Quart. J. Econ.,* 64:319–327 (May 1950).

centers, each complete, offering employment, shopping, entertainment, et cetera, and each with a loyal population, so that one of the givens of the problem is what population will be oriented to which center. This was the problem considered above, which yielded solutions parallel to those of agricultural theory in the case of a multiplicity of markets. A second meaning would be that of competing, complete centers, but centers which did not have a loyal population. That is to say, from the point of view of an individual,

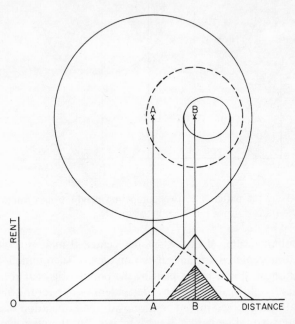

FIGURE 40. Rent patterns of two competing neighboring centers of unequal size

these centers would be alternative, and he would choose that which suited him best. There would be no problem in finding the equilibrium solution of the individual: it would involve the comparison of the optimal locations with respect to each of the two centers. But a market solution would be more complicated, since each individual would be bidding in the land market of both centers, but settling in only one or the other. This type of problem can probably be handled, but the assumption that the income of the individual is known would become questionable under these circumstances. Moreover, if the urban firms are also allowed their choice of centers, the assumptions become untenable, since the volume of business function for the firm depends largely upon the distribution of the population[50] and since the location of these firms determines the employment, shopping, and other facilities at the competing centers, thus determining the relative attractiveness of these centers for the population.[51] Therefore, one could not validly regard as "given" the income and tastes of the individual or the volume of business and operating costs equations of the firm.

A third interpretation of the words "competing centers," that of complementary centers, is of great interest. In such a case, there might be a variety of centers (one or more retail centers, financial centers, manufacturing centers, et cetera) which are separated in space.[52] Different people might be differently oriented toward these centers, and this would be reflected both in their utility and in their commuting costs functions. A number of distances, t_1, t_2, et cetera, would have to be considered, each corresponding to the distance to one of these centers, rather than the single distance t to the all-purpose center of the simpler case. The solution of individual equilibrium would be complicated by a greater number of equations, one additional one for every center, and the geometrical problems would become more complex. However, a solution of individual equilibrium should be possible. Market equilibrium is more problematical. A chain of marginal and equilibrium price-locations would exist, but bid price curves would not suffice for the analysis: the full, complex surfaces of bid prices would have to be considered, and it is questionable whether a systematic method for establishing the chain could be found. When faced with an empirical problem, however, where the population has been divided into relatively few groups, trial and error might suffice to find the solution.

Let us consider a problem of prediction for a city with a variety of complementary centers. We are given the future population of

50. Again, we have the retail or wholesale firm in mind. Other firms may or may not be affected by their proximity to complementary land uses.

51. Wingo, in *Transportation and Urban Land*, outlines an approach to handle some of these interdependences in his model, based on wages being determined by the marginal productivity of labor.

52. See Harris and Ullman, *The Annals*, 242:7–17, for a discussion of the "poly-nucleated city."

the city, divided into groups such as those outlined in the preceding section, and we are also given the location of the various centers.[53] The central activities are classified into some small number w of classifications. Maintaining the same classification of activities and population groups, we find the bid price surface mapping for each group by finding the regressions for the equilibrium bid price surfaces of every group, g, of some form $p_g(t_1, t_2, \ldots, t_w)$[54] in each of several cities. Thus, a bid price function mapping for each group can be prepared which does not depend on any given spatial distribution of the central activities. Such a mapping would serve as well for the single-center case, where all distances, $t_1 \ldots t_w$ will be equal at every location, as for the case in which the central activities are distributed in a number of centers. This general mapping of bid prices could be expressed graphically if only two categories of central activities were being considered, there being three dimensions (p_g, t_1, t_2). However, if more than two central activities are being considered, more than three dimensions would be required and the mapping could not be represented graphically. It would have to remain in the form of regression equations.[55] However, for the city for which we want to predict, where the location of the centers is known, the general mapping would be translated into a mapping of contour lines of equal bid prices over the area of the city.[56] All of the elements necessary for a market solution would then be at hand, and it may be possible to find it by systematic trial and error methods if not too many groups are considered.

The solution resulting from the spatial separation of central

53. It is not necessary that all of one central activity be at the same center. If an activity is distributed between two or more centers, the distance from a point to that activity will be some weighted average of the distances from that point to those centers. In some cases it might be desirable to handle these centers as mutually exclusive alternatives, but see the discussion earlier in this chapter for some of the difficulties this would involve.

54. At the same time, the corresponding regressions for the size of the lot for that group should be found: $q_g(t_1, t_2, \ldots t_w)$.

55. To identify higher and lower bid price functions for the same group, any vector of t's may be chosen, and the bid prices calculated from the various regression equations of that group.

56. A similar approach may be found in Walter G. Hansen, "How Accessibility Shapes Land Use," *J. Amer. Inst. of Planners*, 25:73–76 (May 1959). In a study of Washington, D.C., Mr. Hansen evolves a model in which the "potential" (in the terms of social physics) of an area in terms of its accessibility to a variety of centers of employment, shopping, and population is related to residential development.

activities will not be a simple annular arrangement. For instance, if the upper-income groups are oriented more strongly toward the office and shopping centers than are the lower-income groups, they will have larger absolute values for the regression coefficients of the distances to these centers. The lower-income groups, on the other hand, may be expected to be more strongly oriented toward the centers of manufacturing employment, and the regression coefficient of this distance will presumably be larger in absolute value for these groups. The type of results that might be obtained under these conditions are illustrated in Figures 41 and 42. At point *A* is an

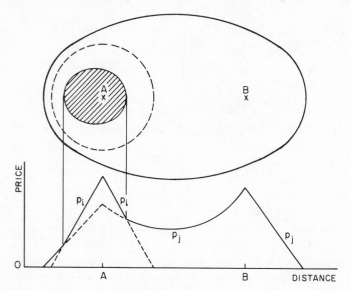

FIGURE 41. A possible rent and occupancy pattern for two complementary centers: an island of high-income population

However, Mr. Hansen's approach does not use the intermediate variable of land prices or a subdivision of the population. The work of others in the area of gravity and potential models (see, for instance, John R. Hamburg and Roger L. Creighton, "Predicting Chicago's Land Use Pattern," *J. Amer. Inst. of Planners*, 25:67–72 [May 1959], and John Q. Stewart and William Warntz, "Physics of Population Distribution," *J. of Regional Science*, 1:99–123 [Summer 1958]) suggests that the form of the regressions of bid price might take a form similar to that of these models. That is to say, using the inverse of some power of the distances $t_1, t_2, \ldots, t_w$ with a positive coefficient.

office and shopping center, and at *B* a manufacturing center. Some of the population both shops and works at *A*, and has a bid price function such as p_i in the lower part of the figures. The rest of the population works at *B* but shops at *A*, and has a twin-peaked bid price surface such as p_j, focused around both centers. The map distribution of the population is shown diagrammatically in the upper part of the figures. The shaded areas are occupied by those who both work and shop at *A*.

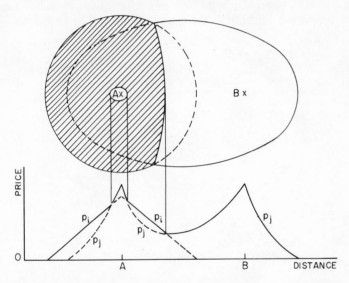

FIGURE 42. A possible rent and occupancy pattern for two complementary centers: populations side by side and an island of low income

If factors such as status symbols are considered, this type of analysis can generate a "sector theory" similar to that of H. Hoyt.[57] Suppose that the lower-income population of city A has a bid price surface such as p_i in Figure 43. The upper-income groups, which are assumed to have less steep bid price surfaces (see section C of this chapter), are also assumed to be concerned with prestige and to wish to associate principally among themselves. Consequently, they take into account their distance from some focus of social life as

57. Homer Hoyt, "The Structure and Growth of Residential Neighborhoods in American Cities," F.H.A., 1939.

well as their distance from the center of the city. If they were distributed in a thin ring at the periphery of the city, these higher-income groups would be dissatisfied with the difficulty of interaction with people of their own class and with the absence of the status derived from living in a well-defined prestige area. We have

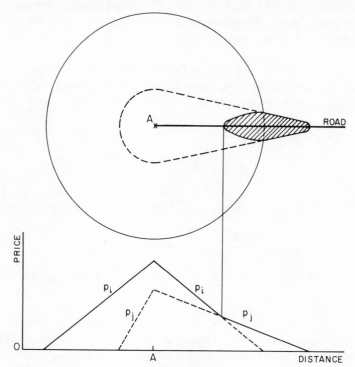

FIGURE 43. Rent and occupancy patterns for a city with a center and a high-status road

assumed, for the purposes of illustration, that the rich will choose to concentrate about a road radial from the center of the city.[58] Their

58. The example is suggested by the Philadelphia Main Line. Hoyt notes: "In all cities studied the high grade residential area had its point of origin near the retail and office center. This is where the higher income groups work . . ." (*ibid.*, p. 116). He notes that the sector of upper class residences moves along existing lines of travel toward high ground and open country. Thus, the choice of a road as the focus is in general agreement with Hoyt's observations, which in part answer the question of which road should be the focus.

desire to be close to this road will be reflected in their utility functions, in which distance from the road will produce disutility. As a
result, their bid price surface will not be radially symmetrical about
the center of the city, but greatly elongated along the axis of the
road, as curve p_j in the lower part of Figure 43. The shape of this
bid price surface, p_j, is also shown in three dimensions in Figure 44.
The resulting distribution of population is shown in the upper part
of Figure 43, where the area occupied by the higher-income group
is shaded.

It should be noted that Hoyt explains the peripheral location of
high-income sectors by a dynamic process of obsolescence of the
older and more central structures, and the building of new ones

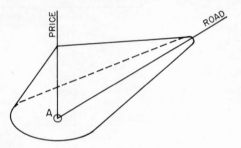

FIGURE 44. Bid price surface, p_j, of the high-income group shown in
Figure 43

further out along the same route. Thus, according to Hoyt, the
high-income sector moves outward by a process of regeneration
over time, aided by the increase of population which takes over the
abandoned older structures. In our theory, a static process produces
not only a sector, but a peripheral one without recourse to the
passage of time. Moreover, as population grows, or the general level
of income increases, or transportation improves, the effect of
change over time according to our theory would be to move the
sector outward as a result of changes in land prices rather than as a
result of the obsolescence of structures (cf. section C, this chapter).
This is in accordance with Hoyt's morphological observations, but
the explanatory theory is different.

APPENDIXES

A

A Simultaneous Equations Solution

1. INTRODUCTION

A simultaneous equations solution has, over an iterative solution, the advantage of elegance and neatness. The solution to be outlined below has the further advantages of minimizing some of the inconsistencies arising from the "extended point" assumptions of the iterative model (for example, the jump-discontinuous curve of the price structure). However, as will be seen below, the simultaneous equations approach presented here presupposes that an approximation to the solution has already been found by the iteration model presented in chapter 5, and may best be viewed as a short-cut for further approximation to a numerical solution in place of repeated iterations.

The problem of the "extended point" is probably the principal reason for the independent development of the theories of agricultural and industrial (i.e., manufacturing) location theory. The former is forced to consider spatial extension, whereas the latter retains the point-location assumption. Cf. Dunn, *The Location of Agricultural Production* for a comparison of the two theories, in particular his observation that agricultural theory applies to the industry as a whole, while manufacturing location theory is a theory of the firm.

2. LOCATION AND AREA OCCUPIED: INDIVIDUAL EQUILIBRIUM

It will be remembered from chapter 2 that when we solved for the individual faced by a given price structure, we assumed that he settled at a point. However, when we considered the effect of the interaction of individuals on the price structure, we had to treat the spatial extension of their holdings. This has been the origin of some inconsistency: the point of location has no dimension, whereas we have had to consider areas, and consequently have had to expand these points of location. The requirement of tangency of the bid price curve to the price structure implies tangency *at a point*. If we accept the fact that occupancy requires spatial extension, it becomes clear that the price obtained by such tangency is in reality the *mean value* of the price structure over the area occupied.

Consider the matter in its formal terms. Expenditure for land is the integral of price over area,

$$\int_{t_i}^{t_{i+1}} P(t)dS, \quad \text{or} \quad \int_{t_i}^{t_{i+1}} P(t)(dS/dt)dt.$$

(The individual's lot is here considered as ring-shaped. The location t_i is that of the individual, and t_{i+1} that of the next individual away from the center.) We have been equating $q_i p_i = \int_{t_i}^{t_{i+1}} P(t)dS$. Since $q_i = \int_{t_i}^{t_{i+1}} dS$ (of which $q_i = S(t_{i+1}) - S(t_i)$ is the solution), we can see that p_i (the equilibrium price paid by the individual in the interaction solution of chapter 5) is the mean value of $P(t)$ in this area. This follows since $p_i = \int P(t)dS / \int dS = $ total value/area $=$ average price per areal unit. Thus, the horizontal segments $p_1, p_2, \ldots p_n$ of the price structure obtained from the iteration solution would be the mean values of the corresponding segments of a continuous price structure. Graphically, a continuous $P(t)$ would run through the horizontal segments of a discontinuous price structure, approximately bisecting them.

There is another simplification we have made because of this inconsistency. The individual buying land is implicitly assumed to be buying it at his rear (that is, he locates at the point of his property nearest the center of the city, and increases in his land holdings are away from the center). Therefore, the marginal cost of land is not the price of land at his point of location, t_i, but the price of land at the point of his property farthest away from his front door, t_{i+1}.

Let us solve now for individual equilibrium making these considerations explicit. We must now make clear which t we mean, since we are allowing for the extension of the individual's property. We specify t_i as the distance from the center of the city to the front line of the lot, and t_{i+1} as the distance to the rear of the lot. Rewriting the basic equations for the individual we have:

(A:1) $$u = u(t_i, q, z)$$

(A:2) $$y = p_z z + \int_{t_i}^{t_{i+1}} P(t)(dS/dt)dt + k(t).$$

We maintain the concentric rings arrangement for individual property so that

(A:3) $$q = \int_{t_i}^{t_{i+1}} dS = S(t_{i+1}) - S(t_i);$$

and from this, the derivative is

(A:4) $$dq = [dS(t_{i+1})/dt]/dt_{i+1} - [dS(t_i)/dt]/dt_i.$$

Now we proceed as usual, maximizing utility within the budget restriction. The process is somewhat complicated by the integrals, but remains basically unchanged.

The differential of the utility function (A:1), when utility is maximized so that $du=0$, will be:

(A:5) $$0 = du = u_{t_i} dt_i + u_q dq + u_z dz.$$

Substituting for dq in equation (A:5) from equation (A:4);

(A:6) $$0 = u_{t_i} dt_i + u_q[dS(t_{i+1})/dt]/dt_{i+1} - u_q[dS(t_i)/dt]dt_i + u_z dz.$$

To find the individual's location, we hold $dq=0$ in equation (A:5) as we have done before (see chapter 2):

$$du = 0 = u_{t_i} dt_i + u_z dz,$$

which may be rewritten as

(A:7) $$u_{t_i}/u_z = -dz/dt_i.$$

Now, since q is being held constant so that $dq=0$, from equation (A:4) it follows:

(A:8) $$dt_{i+1} = [dS(t_i)/dt][dt/dS(t_{i+1})]dt_i.$$

The budget balance equation (A:2) can be differentiated into:

(A:9) $$0 = dy = p_z dz + d\int_{t_i}^{t_{i+1}} P(t)(dS/dt)dt + [dk(t_i)/dt]dt_i.$$

The expression $d\int_{t_i}^{t_{i+1}} P(t)(dS/dt)dt$ in equation (A:9) may be regarded as having both the upper and the lower limits as variables, becoming

(A:10) $d\int_{t_i}^{t_{i+1}} P(t)(dS/dt)dt$

$$= P(t_{i+1})[dS(t_{i+1})/dt]dt_{i+1} - P(t_i)[dS(t_i)/dt]dt_i.$$

Therefore, the differential of the budget balance equation (A:9) becomes, from substitution from (A:10):

(A:11) $0 = dy = p_z\,dz + P(t_{i+1})[dS(t_{i+1})/dt]dt_{i+1}$

$$- P(t_i)[dS(t_i)/dt]dt_i + (dk/dt)dt_i.$$

Since we are holding $dq = 0$, we may substitute for dt_{i+1} in equation (A:11) from equation (A:8):

$$0 = p_z\,dz + P(t_{i+1})[dS(t_{i+1})/dt][dS(t_i)/dt][dt/dS(t_{i+1})]dt_i$$

$$+ P(t_i)[dS(t_i)/dt]dt_i + [dk(t_i)/dt]dt_i.$$

This reduces to:

(A:12) $0 = p_z\,dz + ([P(t_{i+1}) - P(t_i)]dS(t_i)/dt + dk(t_i)/dt)dt_i.$

from which, rewriting and combining with (A:7):

(A:13) $u_{t_i}/u_z = \dfrac{[dS(t_i)/dt][P(t_{i+1}) - P(t_i)] + dk(t_i)/dt}{p_z}.$

This is quite similar to the relation we found in chapter 2, where equation (2:15) stated $u_t/u_z = (q\,dP/dt + dk/dt)/p_z$. The only difference lies in the first term of the numerator of the right-hand fraction. In the earlier version this represented the marginal change in the cost of land of moving dt distance away from the center (holding quantity constant), and it was equal to the change in price times the quantity of land. In the present version, the change in the cost of moving back dt distance is equal to the difference between the front and rear prices, $P(t_{i+1}) - P(t_i)$, converted into value terms by multiplication by the quantity of land which has changed price, dS/dt. That is, the resident, in moving dt away from the center of the city, will buy $P(t_i)dS/dt$ less of land (in dollar terms), and $P(t_{i+1})dS/dt$

more of land (in dollar terms), while maintaining the quantity of land constant. The similarity between the two expressions will be explored further below. (See also appendix B.)

We have found the solution to the problem of location, but this is only a partial solution to the problem of individual equilibrium. We must now find the partial solution for the quantity of land, q, bought by the individual. To this purpose we hold his location, t_i, constant, so that $dt_i = 0$. We then have, from the maximization of satisfaction in equation (A:6), and holding $dt_i = 0$:

(A:14) $$0 = 0 + u_q[dS(t_{i+1})/dt]dt_{i+1} - 0 + u_z \, dz,$$

which may be rewritten as

(A:15) $$u_q/u_z = -dz/[dS(t_{i+1})/dt]dt_{i+1}.$$

The partial derivative of the budget balance equation (A:2), when $dt_i = 0$, becomes, from equation (A:11):

$$dy = 0 = p_z \, dz + P(t_{i+1})[dS(t_{i+1})/dt]dt_{i+1} + 0 + 0,$$

which may be rewritten as

(A:16) $$-dz/[dS(t_{i+1})/dt]dt_{i+1} = P(t_{i+1})/p_z,$$

so that, by combining equations (A:15, 16), we obtain

(A:17) $$u_q/u_z = P(t_{i+1})/p_z.$$

This is as expected: the consumer buys of a good until its marginal utility is in the same ratio to the marginal utility of the *numéraire* good as the marginal costs of the two goods. The composite good z retains its constant price p_z, but the good land, even at a fixed location, has a varying marginal price, equal to the price at the outer edge of the property, $P(t_{i+1})$.

We are now in the position to solve the problem of individual equilibrium, which presents the four unknowns, t_i, t_{i+1}, q, and z. The problem can be solved on the basis of the four simultaneous equations:

(A:2) $$y = p_z z + \int_{t_i}^{t_{i+1}} P \, dS + k(t_i),$$

(A:13) $$u_{t_i}/u_z = \frac{[dS(t_i)/dt][P(t_{i+1}) - P(t_i)] + dk(t_i)/dt}{p_z},$$

(A:17) $$u_q/u_z = P(t_{i+1})/p_z,$$

(A:3) $$q = S(t_{i+1}) - S(t_i).$$

3. EQUILIBRIUM OF THE MARKET

If we could find the continuous function $P(t)$ resulting from the interaction of the multitude of individuals bidding against each other, we would be able to solve for the market as a whole from the equations for individual equilibrium (A:2, 3, 13, 17). However, this is not possible. We can obtain, as will be shown below, points of the price structure function, but not the function itself.

We know that equations (A:2, 3, 13, 17) will hold for each of the n individuals who constitute the market. Thus we have four equations for each individual and $4n$ equations for all individuals. However, at first glance there appear to be $6n$ unknowns:

Unknown	*Number of equations*
$P(t_i)$	n
$P(t_{i+1})$	n
t_i	n
t_{i+1}	n
q	n
z	n

Total: $6n$

But, since the price at the rear of one individual is the same as the front price of the next individual out, there are not $2n$ prices $P(t_i)$ and $P(t_{i+1})$ to find, but only $n+1$ prices. The same applies to distances t_i and t_{i+1}: there are only $n+1$ of these. Therefore, in reality there are only $4n+2$ unknowns.

We have 4 equations per individual, so that we have $4n$ equations. This is still two short of the number of unknowns. To solve for the unknowns, we must either get rid of more unknowns or find more equations, so that we have the same number of unknowns as equations. Fortunately, we can do just that. The first location available will be occupied, and is a known geographic fact. This gives us the first t_i (namely t_1), thereby reducing the number of unknowns by one. On the other hand, the last price, $P(t_{n+1})$, will be the same as the agricultural price at that location, $P_{ag}(t_{n+1})$, giving us one more equation:

(A:18) $$P(t_{n+1}) = P_{ag}(t_{n+1}).$$

Thus, we have eliminated one unknown, t_1, to bring the number of unknowns down to $4n+1$, and we have added one equation, (A:18), bringing their total to $4n+1$.

Two problems yet remain before we can solve this system of equations. The first is that our budget balance equation (A:2) contains the term $\int_{t_i}^{t_{i+1}} P \, dS$. Since from our system of equations we can only hope to find some points of the function $P(t)$, but cannot derive the function itself, we cannot yet solve the system of equations. However, we may use the approximation

(A:19) $$\int_{t_i}^{t_{i+1}} P(t)dS \sim (\tfrac{1}{2}[P(t_i)+P(t_{i+1})]) \int_{t_i}^{t_{i+1}} dS.$$

which may be rewritten more simply, from equation (A:3), as

$$(\tfrac{1}{2})[P(t_i)+P(t_{i+1})]q.$$

We assume that the mean of the extreme prices is the mean price over the area q. This is a simplification likely to introduce a small error into the solution. However, since we are already using the simplification of concentric rings, we are already dealing with approximations.

The other problem is a deeper one. We have the required number of equations, but we do not know where any individual is located in relation to any other. We have the chain of equations, but do not know the position of the individual links. In other words, to solve the system we must know beforehand the spatial sequence of the individuals from the center outward. Conceivably, one could solve for all possible permutations and choose the one that gives a stable solution, that is, the one in which no individual will prefer to shift his location. This would obviously be impractical as soon as the number of individuals becomes at all large. We have, however, a way of finding this spatial sequence by the iteration method described in chapter 5, provided that we can show that the ordering obtained there is equivalent, or at any rate a close approximation, to the one necessary for equilibrium in the simultaneous equations system we are now considering. It will in fact be such an approximation, within the limits of the assumptions of each method: extended point versus ring-shaped lot.

In the iteration model we proceeded by finding the requirements for the equilibrium of an individual when faced by a given price structure, and then constructing a price structure such that the requirements for equilibrium of all individuals are satisfied. In finding this price structure we found a spatial ordering of the individuals in the form of a chain of marginal and equilibrium price-locations. In the present simultaneous equations model we have described the equilibrium requirements of the individual. However, because of the nature of simultaneous equations, we cannot find at the same time the price structure and the spatial ordering of individuals. We must have the latter to obtain the former. If we can show that the equilibrium requirements of the individual *vis à vis* the price structure are equivalent in the two models, we may expect the two solutions to be similar, each within its limits as an approximation to the other. Since the solutions by the two methods would then be similar, the spatial ordering of individuals obtained in the iteration model may be taken as a close approximation to a satisfactory ordering of individuals for the solution of the simultaneous equations model. The simultaneous equations model has been built in such a way that, by considering the spatial extension of the individual's property, it is more sensitive to his marginal conditions (cf. equation (A:17)). It cannot, however, generate its own spatial ordering of individuals. The iteration model is less accurate but sturdier and able to generate its own ordering. We can view, then, the iteration model as a first approximation, principally designed to provide this ordering. The spatial ordering of individuals is then plugged into the simultaneous equations model for a more accurate solution.

To repeat, then, if we can show that the individual requirements for equilibrium are equivalent (that is, close approximations) between the two models, we will have gone a long way toward proving that the ordering obtained in one can be used in the other. Further, if we can show that the principle of spatial ordering, based on the relation between neighbors, is equivalent, the proof will be stronger. However, the proof cannot be complete, for we are dealing with approximations, and it is always possible that very small differences will prove significant.

The principal requirements with reference to the ordering of individuals is, of course, their spatial location. In the iteration model we had the requirement that

(2:15) $$u_t/u_z = (q\ dP/dt + dk/dt)/p_z;$$

in the simultaneous equations we have:

(A:13) $$u_{t_i}/u_z = \frac{[dS(t_i)/dt][P(t_{i+1}) - P(t_i)] + dk(t_i)/dt}{p_z}.$$

Since in these two equations everything but the first term of the numerator of the right-hand side is identical, if we can show the equivalence of $q\ dP/dt$ to $[dS(t_i)/dt][P(t_{i+1}) - P(t_i)]$, we will have shown the two conditions to be equivalent.

First, let us recall the definition of q,

(A:3) $$q = S(t_{i+1}) - S(t_i).$$

Let us define:

(A:20) $$q \equiv \Delta S = S(t_{i+1}) - S(t_i)$$

(A:21) $$\Delta P \equiv P(t_{i+1}) - P(t_i)$$

(A:22) $$\Delta t \equiv t_{i+1} - t_i.$$

The question, then, may be stated as:

$$\Delta S(dP/dt) \overset{?}{\sim} (dS/dt)\Delta P.$$

From the definition of a derivative,

(A:23) $$\Delta S/\Delta t \sim dS/dt.$$

From the approximation described in (A:23), we may say that

(A:24) $$(dS/dt)\Delta P \sim (\Delta S/\Delta t)\Delta P = \Delta S(\Delta P/\Delta t).$$

Again, from the definition of a derivative,

(A:25) $$\Delta P/\Delta t \sim dP/dt.$$

Therefore, from (A:24, 25):

$$(dS/dt)\Delta P \sim \Delta S(dP/dt).$$

The two expressions are therefore equivalent.

We have now shown that the conditions for the location of the individual faced with a given price structure are equivalent in these two models. It will be recalled that in the iteration model we showed, from this condition for the location of the individual, and by using the concept of the bid price curve, that individuals were ordered from the center outward in order of decreasing steepness of their bid price curves. Since the price structure in that model is a composite of segments of the bid price curves of all individuals, this is equivalent to saying that the price structure is steeper than the bid price curve of an individual toward the center (from his location), and less steep away from the center. If we can show that an equivalent condition is necessary for equilibrium in the simultaneous equations solution, we will then have shown that the principle of spatial ordering of individuals is the same in the two models. If this can be shown, then the simultaneous equations model may borrow the spatial ordering of individuals from the iteration model, and this ordering will be accurate within the limits of the approximation.

Let us assume that an individual i moves a very small distance dt from his equilibrium location at t_i, so that the individual is located at $t_i + dt$. This movement dt is so small (it can be made as close to zero as desired), that u_t/u_z, dS/dt, and dk/dt do not change; that is to say:

$$(A:26) \quad u_t(t_i, z_i, q_i)/u_z(t_i, z_i, q_i) = u_t([t_i + dt], q_i, z_i)/u_z([t_i + dt], q_i, z_i),$$

$$(A:27) \qquad\qquad dS(t_i)/dt = dS(t_i + dt)/dt,$$

$$(A:28) \qquad\qquad dk(t_i)/dt = dk(t_i + dt)/dt.$$

It was proved above that an individual is in equilibrium (that he will not move from that location) when

$$(A:13) \quad u_t/u_z = \frac{[dS(t_i)/dt][P(t_{i+1}) - P(t_i)] + dk(t_i)/dt}{p_z}.$$

On the other hand, he will move toward the center if the ratio of the marginal costs exceeds the marginal rate of substitution:

$$(A:29) \quad u_t/u_z < \frac{[dS(t_i')/dt][P(t_{i+1}') - P(t_i')] + dk(t_i')/dt}{p_z}.$$

In inequality (A:29), t_i' is greater than the equilibrium location t_i.

If we consider a location t_i' very close to the equilibrium location t_i, we may write $t_i + dt$ instead of t_i'. Then, from (A:14, 29), it follows that:

(A:30) $\quad \dfrac{[dS(t_i)/dt][P(t_{i+1}) - P(t_i)] + dk(t_i)/dt}{p_z}$

$$< \frac{[dS(t_i + dt)/dt][P(t_{i+1} + dt) - P(t_i + dt)] + dk(t_i + dt)/dt}{p_z}.$$

We can extract the source of the inequality in (A:30):

(A:31) $\qquad P(t_{i+1}) - P(t_i) < P(t_{i+1} + dt) - P(t_i + dt).$

Since the price after the small change in distance dt is equal to the original price plus a small change in price, dP, the terms on the right-hand side of inequality (A:31) may be rewritten as:

(A:32) $\qquad\qquad P(t_{i+1} + dt) = P(t_{i+1}) + dP(t_{i+1}),$

(A:33) $\qquad\qquad P(t_i + dt) = P(t_i) + dP(t_i).$

Substituting equations (A:32, 33) into inequality (A:31), we obtain:

(A:34) $\quad P(t_{i+1}) - P(t_i) < P(t_{i+1}) + dP(t_{i+1}) - P(t_i) - dP(t_i).$

Subtracting the right-hand side of inequality (A:34) from both sides, we obtain:

$$0 < dP(t_{i+1}) - dP(t_i),$$

which may be rewritten as

(A:35) $\qquad\qquad dP(t_i) < dP(t_{i+1}).$

Dividing both sides of (A:35) by dt yields

(A:36) $\qquad\qquad dP(t_i)/dt < dP(t_{i+1})/dt.$

Since $dP/dt < 0$, it follows from (A:36) that $|dP(t_i)/dt| > |dP(t_{i+1})/dt|$, that is, that the price structure is steeper toward the center of the city. The proof that the price structure is less steep away from the center parallels this proof. It follows that, when the market is in equilibrium, the ranking of individuals by the steepness of the slope of their segment of the price structure corresponds to their spatial ranking by distance from the center of the city. This is what we wanted to prove to justify the transferring to this model of the spatial ordering of individuals obtained in the iteration model.

It cannot be concluded, from the proof given, that the price structure will be convex toward the origin, though this is a strong likelihood. The inequalities apply only to the neighborhood of the equilibrium location of the individual. What we have done, in effect, is to assume the segment of the individual's bid price curve in the neighborhood of his equilibrium location to be straight. While the assumption is valid in the neighborhood of his equilibrium location, it would not be valid to assume that inequalities such as (A:36) are transitive without limit, and therefore that the price structure must be less and less steep as it moves away from the center of the city. For instance, if all the bid price curves are concave toward the origin, the resulting price structure might also be concave.

Once the simultaneous equations solution has been worked through, a complete test of the stability of the market equilibrium requires that every individual should be tested at every location, to see whether he would derive greater satisfaction at any other than that which, according to the solution, is his equilibrium location. Or, as a short cut, by way of approximation, a bid price curve may be drawn for each individual,

$$p_i(t) [\![t_i, \bar{p}_i$$

where $p_i(t)$ is the bid price curve for individual i which passes through point $t_i, \bar{p}_i$; t_i is the individual's location, and $\bar{p}_i$ is the mean price he pays:

$$\bar{p}_i = \left(\int_{t_i}^{t_{i+1}} P \, dS \right) / q.$$

Since $P(t_i) > \bar{p}_i > P(t_{i+1})$, this bid price curve will *not* be tangent at t_i, but just below the $P(t)$ curve. The test should be made to determine that

$$P(t) - p_i(t) [\![t_i, \bar{p}_i \geqslant P(t_i) - p_i(t_i) [\![t_i, \bar{p}_i.$$

That is to say, one may test to see whether the equilibrium bid price curve of the individual is closest to the price structure at his equilibrium location. Of course, the bid price curve should never rise above the price structure if the market is in equilibrium. The test suggested will reveal such an inconsistency.

If slight discrepancies appear, individuals could be moved backward or forward in the spatial ordering until a satisfactory solution is achieved. However, these adjustments would probably be unnecessary, or at any rate minor, since they would only arise from the inaccuracies of the approximations made. Moreover, even if discrepancies are allowed to remain without correction, they are likely to have only small effects on the price structure or on the magnitude of the distance of location. These errors would tend to cancel out. Suppose two individuals are transposed, so that the individual we have ranked $i+1$th should really be the ith individual, and *vice versa*. The individual we have called $i+1$th would buy more land in our solution than he would in his proper (ith) location, since he would be on cheaper land. However, the individual we called ith would buy less land in his proper location ($i+1$th). Similarly, the steepness of the price curve we would obtain from our so-called $i+1$th individual would be greater than that of the real $i+1$th individual at the same location. However, the so-called ith individual will give his section of the price curve a gentler slope than would the real ith individual. Consequently, these errors would tend to cancel out, and the total effect would be small.

B

The Shape of the Individual Lot

1. INTRODUCTION

In chapter 5, section G, it was said that, in our model, the lot of the individual possessed the attribute of size (q) but not that of shape. In this appendix we shall reconsider the problem of individual equilibrium including the shape of the lot. As will be seen below, the problem can be solved, though the mathematics of it are quite complicated. This complexity is such that it makes improbable a market solution which considers more realistically shaped lots. Such a market solution is not attempted here. Rather, we shall explore individual equilibrium in terms of its components. First, we shall consider the location as given and solve for the size and shape of the lot; later, we shall consider the problem of location when the shape of the lot is a variable.

2. THE SHAPE OF THE LOT

The consumer, we have said, cares about three things: his location (t), the amount of land he possesses (q), and the amount of all other goods he enjoys (z). His preferences are represented by his utility function (2:2) $u(z, q, t)$. However, let us examine more closely the concept of the quantity of land the individual holds. An annular plot may be a ribbon one half inch deep and twenty miles in circumference, a shape which is thoroughly unusable. It would suit the individual much better to have a lot of 44×100 feet, which would cover the same area. Here is the crux of the problem. The individual cares not only about the quantity of land, q, but he also cares about the shape of the lot. The question of the shape of the lot may be restated as concerning the individual's accessibility from his front door to the more distant corners of his lot. This is a repetition of the problem of accessibility, but seen this time through a microscope. By regarding only the quantity of land, we have ignored the preference of the individual for a shape that minimizes the periphery of his lot with respect to its area. The analysis below will examine this force toward condensation.

We can no longer say that the preference of the individual is described by the utility function (2:2) $u(z, q, t)$. Rather, it is described by the more complicated utility function

(B:1) $$u(z, t, v),$$

where v is a function not only of quantity of land (q), but also of the shape of the lot, that is, of the location of this land with respect to the individual's front door. That is, a small increase in the quantity of land held by the individual (dq) will have to be weighted by some function of its distance from the front door. This weighted measure of quantity will be equal to a small increase dv in the function v, which is the combined measure of area and shape of the lot. This may be expressed formally in mathematical terms. Let us call the distance from dq to the front door h, and the way this distance is used to weight dq we shall call $f(h)$. The function $f(h)$ is thus a variety of utility function, indicating the individual's relative preference (weight) for land near or distant to his front door. The function $f(h)$ will decrease with increases in h (that is, $df/dh < 0$), to represent the individual's greater preference for land near his front door to more distant land. The increase in land quantity, dq, weighted by the function of its position relative to the individual's front door, $f(h)$, is the increase dv:

(B:2) $$dv = f(h)dq.$$

The total weighted "value" of the lot, v, to the individual (that is, the combination of shape and size) will be the integral of equation (B:2):

(B:3) $$v = \int f(h)dq.$$

(The similarity of this approach to that of potential models is obvious. The function v is the autopotential of his own lot. That is, $v = \lim_{\Delta q \to 0} \Sigma \Delta q f(h) = \int f(h)dq$, where h is the distance from a point to the front door, and where $df/dh < 0$. Most potential models use a form of the function $f(h)$ where $f(h) = h^{-\alpha}$, there being much debate as to the proper exponent α. However, I shall retain the more general form $f(h)$, where $df/dh < 0$. In this view the individual treats his lot-potential, v, as one of his goods, and tries to maximize the satisfaction derived from this good *vis à vis* the other goods with reference to their marginal costs.) When we differentiate the revised utility function (B:1), we obtain:

$$du = u_z \, dz + u_t \, dt + u_v \, dv,$$

which by substitution from equation (B:2) becomes

(B:4) $$du = u_z \, dz + u_t \, dt + u_v f(h) dq.$$

From the maximizing conditions, $du = 0$, and, since we are considering size and shape rather than location of lot, $dt = 0$. Equation (B:4) may then be rewritten as

(B:5) $$-dz/dq = u_v f(h)/u_z.$$

The individual is facing a given price structure, $P(t)$. His budget equation is a revised form of equation (2:1):

(B:6) $$y = p_z z + \int P(t) dq + k(t),$$

where $\int P(t) dq$ is his expenditure for land (the integral of price taken over the area of the lot). Differentiating equation (B:6) we obtain:

(B:7) $$0 = dy = p_z \, dz + d \int P(t) dq + (dk/dt) dt.$$

The differential of land cost is

$$d \int P(t) dq = \left(\delta \int P \, dq/\delta q \right) dq + \left(\delta \int P \, dq/\delta t \right) dt$$
$$= P(t) dq + \left[\int (dP/dt) dq \right] dt.$$

But, since we are holding t constant, so that $dt = 0$, we may write simply:

(B:8) $$d \int P(t) dq = P(t) dq.$$

Substituting equation (B:8) into the differential of the budget balance equation (B:7), we have

(B:9) $$0 = dy = p_z \, dz + P(t)dq + (dk/dt)dt.$$

Holding t constant so that $dt=0$, equation (B:9) may be rewritten:

(B:10) $$-dz/dq = P(t)/p_z.$$

Consequently, from equations (B:5, 10), we obtain:

(B:11) $$f(h)u_v/u_z = P(t)/p_z.$$

Equation (B:11) may also be written as

(B:12) $$u_v/u_z = [P(t)/f(h)]/p_z.$$

Equation (B:12) represents the marginal condition along the periphery of the individual's lot. The marginal rate of substitution, u_v/u_z, is equal to the ratio of the prices of land and the composite good. However, since the quantity of land is weighted according to its accessibility from the front door by multiplying it by the function $f(h)$, the price of land must conversely be weighted by dividing it by the function of its accessibility. Thus, expensive land near the front door and cheap land farther away are, from the point of view of the individual, equivalent.

The condition may be readily understood from Figure 45. The conical shape is $f(h)$ times the marginal equilibrium constant, $(u_v/u_z)p_z$. The reason for this complex form is described below. The flat surface is a portion of the price structure $P(t)$, and the shaded area is the shape of the lot, with area q. The dimension h is measured radially from point t_i, at which the front door is located.

Before the problem could be solved in practice, both distance functions, $P(t)$ and $f(h)$, should be converted to common co-ordinates. Since $P(t)$ is given, the simplest method is to use rectangular co-ordinates r and s, where the individual's location at t_i is $(0, 0)$ and $h = \sqrt{r^2 + s^2}$. We then have $f(\sqrt{r^2 + s^2})$. We can convert $P(t)$ into $P(r, s)$ and then solve for either implicit equation $s(r)$ or $r(s)$. Alternatively, using polar co-ordinates, with the origin at the center of the city, the individual's front door location is given by t_i, θ_i. The function $P(t)$ would not be altered, and the function $f(h)$ would become

$$f(\sqrt{[\sin \theta_i t_i - t \sin \theta]^2 + [t_i \cos \theta_i - t \cos \theta]^2}),$$

which reduces to

$$f(\sqrt{t_i{}^2 + t^2 - 2t_i t[\cos (\theta - \theta_i)]}).$$

From equations (B:11, 12), the complex expression $f(h)(u_v/u_z)p_z$ is seen to equal $P(t)$ at the periphery of the lot. Examination of the

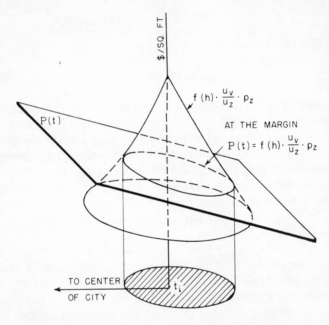

FIGURE 45. Diagrammatic derivation of the shape of the lot

units will reveal it to be a variety of bid price function, that is, how much the individual is willing to pay for land at distance h from his front door. The function $f(h)$, which is used as a weight, is a relative number and has no units. The units of the marginal utility, u_v, are utility per square foot. The units of u_z are utility per unit of z, and the units of p_z are dollars per unit of z. Therefore, the expression

$f(h)(u_v/u_z)p_z$ may be written, if we regard only the units involved, as

$$\text{pure number } \frac{\text{(utility/square feet)}}{\text{(utility/units of } z)} \frac{\text{dollars}}{\text{units of } z}.$$

This reduces to dollars per square foot (a bid price for land). Since these are also the units of the price structure, $P(t)$, the vertical axis in Figure 45 measures both in terms of dollars per square foot. Figure 45 permits us to see the basic shape that results. Over this small area $P(t)$ has been represented by an inclined plane. (This has been done for simplicity. Over a small area, the conic segment of the price structure would approach such an inclined plane.) We obtain an ovoid shape for the lot, with the small end toward the center of the city. Figure 46 shows such a shape, solved for a set of arbitrary specific equations. It will be noted that the greatest width of the lot (in the S dimension) is not at $r = 0$, but at some point behind it, $r > 0$, as is characteristic of the ovoid shape.

Where the price of land, $P(t)$ is a constant over the area of the lot, the resulting shape will be a circle, centered about the front door. Graphically, it would result from a horizontal section across the cone in Figure 45, made by a horizontal $P(t)$. More formally, the circular shape of the lot when price is constant can be deduced from the relation (from equation [B:11])

$$P/f = (u_v/u_z)p_z = \text{constant},$$

so that if P is a constant, f must be a constant.

As the slope of price becomes steeper, the ovoid shape is accentuated. Again, this may be seen graphically from Figure 45 by imagining a clockwise rotation of the $P(t)$ plane. It may also be done mathematically. The distance, r_a, from the front door to the point nearest the center of the city becomes smaller relative to the distance to the farthest point, r_b. If P_0 is the price at the front door, and the slope of the price structure in this area is dP/dt (or dP/dr), price is given by the linear equation $P = P_0 + (dP/dr)r$. We wish to show that the ratio r_b/r_a becomes greater as the price structure increases in steepness, that is, $d(r_b/r_a)/d(dP/dr) > 0$; or, since $\delta f/\delta r < 0$, that $d(f_b/f_a)/d(dP/dr) < 0$. Since P/f is a constant, $P_b/P_a = f_b/f_a = [P_0 - (dP/dr)r_b]/[P_0 - (dP/dr)r_a$, and $d(f_b/f_a)/d(dP/dr) = [P_0(x_a - x_b)]/[P_0 - (dP/dr)r_a]^2$, where x is the directional equivalent of the measure of distance r. Since $P_0 > 0$, $x_a < 0$, and $x_b > 0$, it follows that $d(f_b/f_a)/d(dP/dr) < 0$.

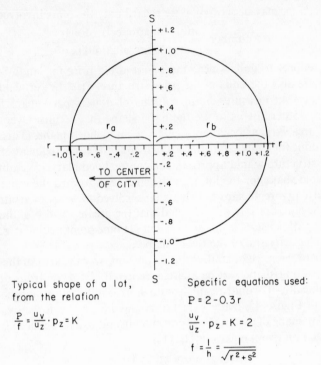

Typical shape of a lot,
from the relation

$$\frac{P}{f} = \frac{u_v}{u_z} \cdot p_z = K$$

Specific equations used:

$$P = 2 - 0.3\,r$$

$$\frac{u_v}{u_z} \cdot p_z = K = 2$$

$$f = \frac{1}{h} = \frac{1}{\sqrt{r^2 + s^2}}$$

FIGURE 46. Typical shape of the lot

3. LOCATION

The problem of the location of the individual in this case is solved in a manner similar to that used when the shape of the lot is not considered, though, of course, the mathematics are more complex. When location and quantity and size are solved for simultaneously, the problem of individual equilibrium has been solved.

Our new basic equations for the individual are

$$(\mathbf{B}{:}1) \qquad u = u(z, t_i, v), \qquad \text{where } v = \int f(h)dq,$$

$$(\mathbf{B}{:}6) \qquad y = p_z z + \int P(t)dq + k(t_i).$$

For clarity, the distance from the center of the city to the front door of the individual will be denoted by t_i, while t will stand for the generic measure of distance from the center of the city at any point.

We wish to find the equilibrium location of the individual. The method is the same used in chapter 2. Differentiating the utility equation (B:2) we obtain

(B:13) $$du = u_z\, dz + u_{t_i}\, dt_i + u_v\, dv.$$

When satisfaction is maximized (that is, $du=0$), holding v constant, so that $dv=0$, we have from (B:13)

(B:14) $$u_{t_i}/u_z = -dz/dt_i.$$

Differentiating the budget balance equation (B:6);

(B:15) $$0 = dy = p_z\, dz + d\int^{\cdot} P(t)dq + (dk/dt)dt_i.$$

The problem is to specify what $d\int P(t)dq$ is. Above, in equation (B:8), we were not concerned with location, so that t_i was considered to be fixed, and $dt_i=0$. However, we must now allow dt_i to vary, and we obtain

(B:16) $$d\int^{\cdot} P(t)dq = \frac{\delta}{\delta q}\left(\int^{\cdot} P(t)dq\right)dq + \frac{\delta}{\delta t_i}\left(\int^{\cdot} P(t)dq\right)dt_i$$
$$= P(t)dq + \left[\int^{\cdot} (dP/dt)dq\right]dt_i.$$

Substituting equation (B:16) into equation (B:15), we obtain

(B:17) $$0 = dy = p_z\, dz + P(t)dq + \left[\int^{\cdot} (dP/dt)dq\right]dt_i + (dk/dt)dt_i.$$

Since we are assuming for the moment $dv=0$, and we defined

(B:2) $$dv = f(h)dq,$$

it follows that $dq=0$.

The differential equation (B:17) may be written, holding $dq=0$,

(B:18) $$-dz/dt_i = \left(\int^{\cdot} [dP(t)/dt]dq + dk/dt\right)/p_z,$$

which, when combined with (B:14), becomes

(B:19) $$u_{t_i}/u_z = \left(\int^{\cdot} [dP(t)/dt]dq + dk/dt\right)/p_z.$$

This is quite similar to the earlier forms

(2:15) $u_t/u_z = (q\,dP/dt + dk/dt)/p_z,$

in the point-location case (see chapter 2), and

(A:13) $u_t/u_z = \dfrac{[dS(t_i)/dt][P(t_{i+1}) - P(t_i)] + dk(t_i)/dt}{p_z}$

in the simultaneous equation solution (see appendix A).

Compare the term $\int[dP(t)/dt]dq$ in equation (B:19) with the term $q(dP/dt)$ in equation (2:15). They may be seen to be equivalent, for the term from equation (B:19) may be rewritten:

$$\int [dP(t)/dt]dq = [dP(t_0)/dt]\int dq = [dP(t_0)/dt]q,$$

where $dP(t_0)/dt$ is the mean value of dP/dt within the region q.

The similarity with the concentric ring form can also be seen. Let us convert the term $\int(dP/dt)dq$ from equation (B:19) into a double integral on the $r-s$ co-ordinates of Figure 46, so that

(B:20) $\displaystyle\int (dP/dt)dq = \int_q\!\!\int (dP/dt)dr\,ds.$

Now, let us integrate along the r-direction only of the double integral of equation (B:20):

$$\int_{t_a}^{t_b} (dP/dt)dr = P(t_b) - P(t_a),$$

where t_a is the distance from the center of the city to the front of the lot, and t_b the distance to the back of the lot. We now complete the operation by integrating along the s direction:

(B:21) $\displaystyle\int [P(t_b) - P(t_a)]ds = \int (dP/dt)dq = \int_q\!\!\int (dP/dt)dr\,ds.$

If we define $[P(\bar{t}_b) - P(\bar{t}_a)]$ as the mean value of $[P(t_b) - P(t_a)]$ in the relevant range, we may rewrite (B:21) as

(B:22) $\displaystyle\int (dP/dt)dq = [P(\bar{t}_b) - P(\bar{t}_a)]\int ds.$

$\int ds$ is the width of the lot, a linear distance equivalent to (dS/dt) in the simultaneous equations formulation. The right-hand side of equation (B:22), $[P(\bar{t}_b) - P(\bar{t}_a)]\int ds$ is therefore equivalent to the term $(P_{t_{i+1}} - P_{t_i})(dS/dt)$ in the simultaneous equation solution.

4. Note on Location by Polar Co-ordinates

For completeness, let us consider the location of the individual as defined in terms of polar co-ordinates originating at the center of the city. The individual is located at (t_i, θ_i). The differential of his utility function, $u(z, v, [t_i, \theta_i])$, will be

$$du = u_z\,dz + u_v\,dv + u_{t_i}\,dt_i + u_{\theta_i}\,d\theta_i.$$

But, as the individual does not care about sectors in the featureless plain, the partial $u_{\theta_i} = 0$. Therefore, holding everything but z and θ_i constant in the differential equation of utility, we obtain

$$u_{\theta_i}/u_z = -dz/d\theta = 0.$$

The budget balance differential equation becomes slightly more complicated. The price structure is now represented by the function $P(t, \theta)$, and we must consider θ as a variable in the expenditure for land $\int P\,dq$. The differential of the budget balance equation (B:6) becomes:

$$dy = 0 = p_z\,dz + P(t)dq + \left[\int (\delta P/\delta t)dq\right]dt_i + \left[\int (\delta P/\delta \theta)dq\right]d\theta + (dk/dt)dt_i.$$

From this, holding everything but z and θ constant,

$$-dz/d\theta = \left[\int (\delta P/\delta \theta)dq\right]/p_z,$$

and

$$u_{\theta_i}/u_z = \left[\int (\delta P/\delta \theta)dq\right]/p_z = 0.$$

Since $u_{\theta_i} = 0$, it follows that $\int(\delta P/\delta \theta)dq = 0$ at equilibrium. This condition is satisfied if price is a function of t only, so that $(\delta P/\delta \theta) = 0$. However, it should be noted that this condition can also be satisfied by any other pattern of $(\delta P/\delta \theta)$ as long as its mean value in the region q is equal to zero.

C

A Regression of Expenditure for Land on Income and Distance

The regression equation cited in chapter 6 provides some evidence of the relevance of the variables used in the theory presented in the body of this work. This appendix is devoted to recounting the method used to establish this empirical equation, with the purpose of illustrating some of the problems encountered in empirical research in this area.

The relationship being tested states that the expenditure for land by a family is determined by their income and their distance from the center of the city. In terms of the notation used above, we may expect some relation:

$$pq = g(y, t).$$

According to our assumptions (see chapter 2), we may expect expenditures for land (pq) to increase with income ($dg/dy > 0$), and to decrease with distance from the center ($dg/dt < 0$). In terms of the linear form of the regression equation, the signs of the regression coefficients should be as follows:

$$pq = a + by - ct.$$

Since data for individual families are not available, it was decided to use average values (per family) of the variables for several areas and to calculate the regression for these synthetic families. While it is true that this approach sins in what has been called "the ecological fallacy" (assuming that a statistical average for a population is typical of its individuals), the choice was limited by the availability of data to using such synthetic families or none at all. The actual unit of observation, then, is the U.S. Census tract. The city studied is Philadelphia, which has the advantage of having its municipal boundaries sufficiently extended to include much of the suburban growth of the metropolitan area. Below is a description of how the several variables were obtained.

1. Expenditure on Land (*pq*)

This is the dependent variable; it was obtained by multiplying the quantity of land per family (*q*) by the price of land per square foot (*p*) for each census tract.

2. Quantity of Land (*q*)

The Philadelphia City Planning Commission (P.C.P.C.) had available figures on the "net residential density" of the census tracts in the city for the year 1950. These figures were calculated by dividing the number of families in a tract (as reported by the 1950 Census) by the "net residential area" of that tract. The "net residential area" was defined (in Philadelphia City Planning Commission, *Residential Densities in Philadelphia*, 1955) as:

the total land area devoted to residential facilities. In areas developed for one family homes, the net residential area will be the land enclosed by the property lines of the lot or sections of continuous lots. Where the residential structure is a multiple dwelling, and part of the surrounding area is used by several families in common, residential facilities will include in addition to the main structure the land used for such necessary auxiliary purposes as administration, maintenance, heating, garages, shops, parking areas, play and recreation areas, but shall exclude vacant unbuildable land. For our purposes, unbuildable land shall include that portion of the property which has a mean gradient of more than 10%.

An unpublished note attached to the land use maps at the P.C.P.C., and used as a directive for the staff in preparing the figures, defined "net residential area" as "all parcels used wholly or predominantly for residential purposes including dwellings with stores; excludes streets, vacant lots, and all other uses." This is obviously a crude measurement involving many decisions based on judgment. However, it was the only such measurement available. Net residential density as calculated by the P.C.P.C. was converted into quantity of land per family (in square feet) by calculating its reciprocal, and multiplying it by the appropriate conversion factor.

It should be noted that, in general, quantity of land per family will be smaller than the average lot size in an area because of the presence of multiple dwelling structures. That is, for instance, if there is a duplex house on a lot, each of the two families is considered to occupy a quantity of land q equal to one half the size of the lot.

3. Price (p)

The P.C.P C. made available a set of some 1,500 cards with the sales price and location of all vacant lots sold in the city during the years 1952 and 1953. The lots were plotted onto P.C.P.C. land use maps and checked to insure (a) that they were located in predominantly residential blocks, to avoid including lots intended for uses other than residential, and (b) that they were in fairly well developed rather than in a predominantly vacant area. This second requirement was intended to exclude lots purchased for development which might be significantly different from that which exists in the area. The area of the lot was obtained directly from the card when available, or measured off the land use map when it was not. The price per square foot was obtained by dividing the sales price of the lot by its area. Where several lots had been sold within one census tract, the mean of their prices was used.

As a rule, the value of a lot is established without explicit reference to any units of measurement; when units of measurement are considered explicitly, these units may be in terms of either frontage in feet or of an areal unit such as square feet. The price paid for the lot, moreover, may be affected by the regularity of its shape and even by its size, so that a larger lot may receive a higher per square foot price than an equivalently located smaller one. However, for simplicity, here price will be price per square foot.

Assessed valuations have been purposely disregarded. It is a common misconception that an assessment constitutes a measure of the intrinsic value of land, while the sales price is subject to transitory vagaries. While it is true that lack of knowledge of the market or some unique circumstances may affect randomly the actual sales price of land, the assessed valuation is required by law, as a rule, to be a best estimate of a likely sales price (or a fixed percentage of that price). Thus, assessed valuation is merely what the assessor's office thinks the land will fetch in the open market.

This opinion is often affected by irrelevant considerations, and is frequently out of date. For these reasons, though assessed valuations are more readily and plentifully available, sales price has been used. The unreliability of the valuation figures may be illustrated from information published in the *Public Information Bulletin No. 3-D(S)* of the P.C.P.C. (1954). The ratio of 1952 sales price of vacant land to its 1953 valuation, by wards, ranged from 0.34 to 1.59. The mean of these ratios was 0.732, and the standard deviation 0.284. It should be noted that the ratios are of aggregate valuation and aggregate assessments for each ward, so that the discrepancies are minimized.

4. INCOME (y)

The median income per family for the tract was used, as reported in the 1950 Census.

5. DISTANCE (t)

Distance was measured in miles in a straight line from the center of the city, which was assumed to be at the intersection of Broad and Market Streets, to the center of the census tract.

There were 402 census tracts in Philadelphia in 1950. Sales in 205 of these were examined. Not all of these tracts had had sales, and many of those which had had them had to be discarded because they did not meet the criteria mentioned above or because there was not enough information given on the card to locate the lot. Only 32 tracts remained, with a total of 52 lots sold.

Expenditure for land per family was computed, and a scatter diagram of expenditure for land against median income was prepared for these tracts. However, no pattern was visible in the diagram.

Reasoning that only areas where the land market had been sufficiently active would exhibit an equilibrium of demand and supply in land values, while in areas where only an occasional lot was sold there would not be sufficient knowledge of the market by buyers or sellers to make the sales price meaningful, the census tracts were separated by their percentage growth in dwelling units from 1940 to 1950. They were formed into two groups: those which had grown by more than 2 per cent (a level which was selected arbitrarily) and those which had grown less than 2 per cent, stayed stable, or actually lost dwelling units. Fifteen of the tracts had grown by more than 2 per cent, and a scatter diagram revealed for these the expected positive relation between income and expenditure. The scatter diagram of the remaining 17 tracts showed no clear relation between these variables, corroborating the assumption. The fifteen tracts that had grown were used in calculating the regression:

$$pq = -222.65 + 0.4357 \, (\pm 0.1275) \, y - 90.107 \, (\pm 22.703) \, t.$$

$$R = 0.6897 \qquad S = 375.67$$

R and S were adjusted for small samples. The variables are: pq, value of land per family; p, price per square foot of land; q, number of square feet per family; y, median income per family; t, distance from the center of the city in miles. Their rounded-off mean values are:

$$\bar{pq} = \$850.00; \quad \bar{y} = \$3,330.00; \quad \bar{t} = 4.0 \text{ miles.}$$

Other forms of the regression were not computed. With only 15 observations, it did not seem justifiable. The usual tests of significance, which refer to the single equation, would not be valid if several forms of the regression were tried, and there would be no way of choosing among the various forms except by picking the one with the highest coefficient of multiple correlation. It is unlikely that the difference would be significant given the small number of cases. Even were a greater number of cases available, the high intercorrelation among the variables makes it unlikely that any one form of the consumption function would be clearly preferable from this type of statistical evidence. In short, the fact that regressions with a coefficient of correlation significantly different from zero are possible encourages the belief that there may be a valid consumption function and that the variables used are important. The method of the synthetic family used here, however, does not clearly indicate the form of the function.

D

Classical Consumer Equilibrium

This appendix is intended for readers who are not thoroughly familiar with the technique. A fuller explanation of the diagrammatic solution may be found in any standard economic textbook, and of the mathematical solution in more advanced ones.

1. DIAGRAMMATIC SOLUTION

Suppose we find out from an individual that he would be equally satisfied with 10 pounds of pears and 5 of apples or with 8 of pears and 6 of apples. We would represent these two combinations by

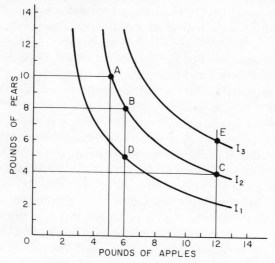

FIGURE 47. Typical indifference curves

points *A* and *B* respectively in Figure 47. If we pursued the matter further, we might learn that he is just as satisfied by having 4 pounds of pears and 12 of apples, represented by point *C*. If we continued asking questions, we could get a great number of such combinations which give him the same satisfaction, and eventually they would fill out to a line such as I_2. The individual would be equally satisfied by all points on the curve, so that he would be indifferent among them. Such a curve, describing combinations of goods among which the individual has no preference, is called an *indifference curve*.

It is assumed in this type of analysis that the individual would rather have more than less of a good. Consequently any point such as D, which gives him the same quantity of apples but less pears than B will be less preferable than B. More generally, any point below an indifference curve will be less preferable than any point on the curve. Thus, if we find the various combinations that afford him the same satisfaction as D and generate another indifference curve (I_1), we can be sure (1) that any point on I_1 is less preferable than any point on I_2, and therefore, (2) that I_1 and I_2 will never cross. Conversely, any curve such as I_3 drawn through a point E above I_2 will be preferable at any point to any point on either I_2 or I_1, and I_3 will never cross with either of the lower curves. In this fashion we could draw a great many such indifference curves and map the tastes of the individual with respect to these two goods.

The assumption that the individual would rather have more than less of a good means that indifference curves will slope downward to the right. Points A and B are equally preferable because what he has lost in pears he has gained in apples. In other words, the individual, if he possessed A apples and pears, could afford to give up 2 pears for one apple without either gaining or losing satisfaction. At any point, the rate at which he is willing to give up one good to gain another is called the *marginal rate of substitution*, and it is represented in the diagram by the slope of the indifference curve at that point. Since he is giving up some of one good to gain some of the other, the slope of the indifference curve must be negative.

It is also assumed that if a consumer has very little of one good, a small increase in the quantity of that good will give him a greater increase in satisfaction than the same small increase in quantity would if he had a great deal of that good. This requirement of *diminishing marginal utility* is part of folklore in the common observation that one dollar difference means a lot more to a poor than to a rich man. This means that at point A, where the individual has many pears and few apples, he will surrender pears for apples more readily than at *C*, where he has many apples and few pears. In other words, the marginal rate of substitution will be greater at *A* than at *C* (if we disregard the sign), and the indifference curve will be steeper at *A* and gentler at *C*, making the curve convex toward the origin.

In summary, an indifference curve map has the following properties:

(a) Higher indifference curves represent more satisfaction than lower ones.

(b) Indifference curves will not cross each other.

(c) They slope downward to the right.

(d) They are convex toward the origin.

In the analysis of residential location in the main text it will be seen that only the first two properties remain true because of the introduction of a good of negative utility, that is, a good of which the individual would rather have as little as possible.

We have so far described only the tastes of the individual. To find out how much of each good he will buy we must find out what combinations of the two goods he can buy with the money he has to

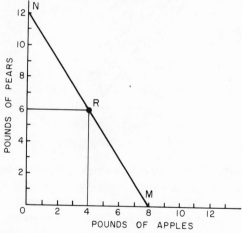

FIGURE 48. Budget line or price-opportunity line

spend. Suppose he has $2.40. Pears cost $0.20 per pound and apples $0.30 per pound. If he spent all of his money on pears he could buy 12 pounds of pears and no apples (point *N* in Figure 48); if he spent it all on apples, he would have 8 pounds of apples and no pears (point *M*). Or he could buy 6 pounds of pears ($1.20) and 4 of apples ($1.20) (point *R*). All the combinations he could buy are represented by the straight line *NM*. Such a line, variously called *budget line, price line,* or *price-opportunity line,* describes *all* of the combinations of the two goods that can be purchased for the amount of money he has to spend. It is a straight line, with the ratio of the two prices (negative) as its slope.

Now we have a description of the combinations available to him; if we join it with the indifference map, which describes his preference pattern, we can tell which combination he will buy. This has been done in Figure 49. The individual will choose the possible point

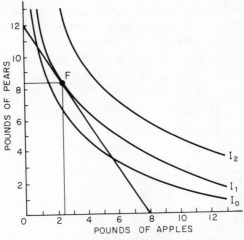

FIGURE 49. Price-opportunity line and indifference curves; equilibrium at *F*

(one on his price-opportunity line) which reaches the highest (most satisfactory) indifference curve to come in contact with his budget line. At this point (*F*), the consumer has maximized his satisfaction within the restraint of his budget. This constitutes the solution to the problem.

It should be noted that at this point the indifference curve must be tangent to the price-opportunity line. If they intersected, it would mean that the price-opportunity curve would come in contact with some higher indifference curve. Tangency means equality of slopes, and therefore the marginal rate of substitution of the two goods is equal to the ratio of their prices. In the body of the book we need a refined version of this statement: that at equilibrium the marginal rate of substitution between two goods is equal to the ratio of their marginal costs. For the time being the distinction is not relevant because in this case marginal cost (the cost of acquiring one more unit of the good) is the same as average cost (total expenditure divided by the number of units purchased) or price.

The same method of analysis can be applied when there are three rather than two goods under consideration. We must deal then with

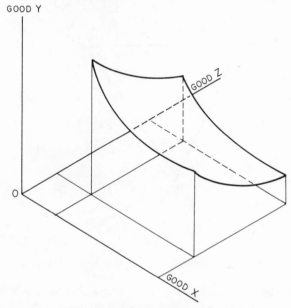

FIGURE 50. An indifference surface

three-dimensional diagrams. The indifference curve becomes an indifference surface convex toward the origin, such as that shown in Figure 50 where goods, *X*, *Y*, and *Z* are being considered. The shape of the curve may be visualized as that of a salad bowl propped up against the corner of a room. It will be noted that the trace of such a surface on a plane parallel to any of the three coordinate planes will be an indifference curve with the shape of that which we obtained from the analysis of the two goods situation.

The budget or price-opportunity line of the two goods case is a surface when three goods are being considered. It is a plane such as *MNR* in Figure 51. The slope of the plane in any direction is the negative of the ratio of the prices of the goods involved. Thus, along *NR*, it will be the ratio of the price of *X* to the price of *Z*; along *MR*, it will be the ratio of the price of *Y* to the price of *X*; and along *MN* it will be the ratio of the price of *Y* to the price of *Z*.

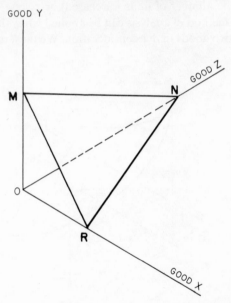

FIGURE 51. Budget or price-opportunity plane

Equilibrium is found at the point where the plane touches the highest indifference surface with which it comes in contact. At this point the surface will be tangent to the plane, and the various marginal rates of substitution (the slope of the indifference surface) will be equal to the price ratios (the slope of the budget plane).

2. MATHEMATICAL SOLUTION

Individual equilibrium may also be described by means of differential calculus. This method has the advantages of greater elegance and of there being no restriction upon the number of goods that may be handled. On the other hand, it does not give the advantage of visualization which the diagrammatic method offers.

Imagine that an individual must choose between n goods $(x_1, x_2, \ldots, x_n)$. His preferences are given by his *utility function*

(D:1) $$u = u(x_1, x_2, \ldots, x_n).$$

This function has the characteristic that increases of any good x_i increase satisfaction (the value of u). In other words, $\delta u/\delta x_i > 0$. The indifference curve of the diagrammatic solution is the representation of $u_0 = u(x_1, x_2)$, where $n=2$ and u_0 is a constant. A higher indifference curve is given by $u_k = u(x_1, x_2)$, where u_k is a constant greater than u_0. The indifference surface is the diagrammatic representation of $u_0 = u(x_1, x_2, x_3)$, where $n=3$. But, whereas diagrammatically we can handle only three goods at the most, there is no limit to the number of goods we can handle mathematically.

The consumer wishes to maximize his satisfaction, u, subject to the restraints of his budget. Once he has spent all his money on some combination of goods he can only acquire more of any good by relinquishing certain amounts of other goods. At the point where his satisfaction has been maximized, the increase in satisfaction derived from increases in any good are nullified by the decrease in satisfaction resulting from the amounts of other goods he must give up. Mathematically, this is expressed by the differential of the utility function (D:1), which will be zero when the function has been maximized. This may be expressed as:

$$0 = du = (\delta u/\delta x_1)dx_1 + (\delta u/\delta x_2)dx_2 + \cdots + (\delta u/\delta x_n)dx_n,$$

where du is the total increase in satisfaction, dx_i, is the increase or decrease of any good x_i, and $\delta u/\delta x_i$ is the increase in satisfaction that would result from a small increase of good x_i. The changes in satisfaction (du) derived from giving up a small amount of any good x_i for a small amount of another good x_j are

$$du = (\delta u/\delta x_i)dx_i + (\delta u/\delta x_j)dx_j.$$

Since u is at a maximum, there can be no further increases of its value and $du = 0$, so that

$$0 = (\delta u/\delta x_i)dx_i + (\delta u/\delta x_j)dx_j,$$

which may also be written as

(D:2) $$(\delta u/\delta x_i)/(\delta u/\delta x_j) = -dx_j/dx_i.$$

The expression $\delta u/\delta x_i$ is the increase in utility derived from a small increase in good x_i, that is, marginal utility. The expression $(\delta u/\delta x_i)/(\delta u/\delta x_j)$ is the ratio of two marginal utilities for a constant (maximum) utility, and thus it is the marginal rate of substitution between the goods x_i and x_j. It is, in terms of the diagrams, the slope of an indifference surface on the x_i–x_j plane.

Let us consider now the budget restriction. The individual has y dollars to spend. The price of good x_1 is p_1, the price of good x_2 is p_2, and so on. He may purchase any combination of the n goods that does not exceed the amount of money y he has to spend. This may be written as

(D:3) $$y = p_1 x_1 + p_2 x_2 + \cdots + p_n x_n.$$

This *budget balance equation* is the budget or price-opportunity line (or surface) of the diagrammatic solution. Differentiating we have

$$dy = (\delta y/\delta x_1)dx_1 + (\delta y/\delta x_2)dx_2 + \cdots + (\delta y/\delta x_n)dx_n.$$

Since y is a constant and cannot increase, $dy=0$. Also, the simple linear form of the equation means that the partial of y with respect to any good is simply the price of that good, so that the differential equation may be rewritten as

$$0 = dy = p_1\,dx_1 + p_2\,dx_2 + \cdots + p_n\,dx_n.$$

If we allow changes only in any two goods, x_i and x_j, y will remain a constant and $dy=0$, so that

$$0 = p_i\,dx_i + p_j\,dx_j.$$

This may be rewritten as

(D:4) $$-dx_j/dx_i = p_i/p_j.$$

This corresponds to our observation in the diagrammatic version that the slope of the price-opportunity line or surface was the negative of the ratio of the prices.

Now we may combine equations (D:2) and (D:4) obtaining

(D:5) $$(\delta u/\delta x_i)/(\delta u/\delta x_j) = p_i/p_j;$$

that is, at equilibrium the marginal rate of substitution is equal to the ratio of the prices. It will be noted that price is the partial derivative of y with respect to the good; that is, $\delta y/\delta x_i = p_i$. This partial derivative is the marginal cost of good x_i, and a more general statement, then, is that at equilibrium the marginal rate of substitution between two goods is equal to the ratio of their marginal costs.

Since there are n goods we may obtain $(n-1)$ independent ratios such as that in equation (D:5). But we have n unknowns ($x_1, x_2, \ldots, x_n$). The budget balance equation (D:3) provides the nth equation. This system of n equations may presumably be solved simultaneously to give us the n unknowns. Thus, we may find how much of each of the n goods the individual will buy to maximize his satisfaction (u) within the restrictions of his budget (y).

E

Lowdon Wingo, Jr.: Transportation and Urban Land

L. Wingo analyzes (in *Transportation and Urban Land* [Washington: Resources for the Future, 1961]) the case of a city with a population homogeneous with respect to income and tastes, and he outlines an approach for the more realistic case of a population in which groups differ in income and taste. In this summary only the simpler case will be presented. The notation used is mine: Mr. Wingo's is similar.

In Mr. Wingo's work, considerable attention is devoted to transport costs. The monetary costs are a function of the distance traveled and terminal costs, which depend on congestion at the center of the city. Transport costs also include the value of the time spent commuting to work. This time is viewed as an extension of working hours, and is priced in dollars according to the marginal value of leisure. These two elements together constitute transport costs, k, which are a function of the distance from the home to the center of the city, t:

$$k(t): \text{ transport costs, in dollars.}$$

Rent for the site is defined simply as the price per unit of area times the quantity of land:

$$pq: \text{ rent,}$$

where p: price per unit of land,
q: quantity of land.

The urban resident views his transport costs and the rent for his site as complementary. Regardless of his location, he will spend the same amount on land rent plus transport costs. This constant amount is equal to the transport costs to the most distant (marginal) residential location, t_m, where the price of land is zero. Therefore this constant will be $k(t_m)$:

(E:1) $$pq + k(t) = k(t_m).$$

Thus, as in Haig's view, rent for land is equivalent to the costs of transport *not* incurred:

(E:2) $$pq = k(t_m) - k(t).$$

The preference for more rather than less land is recognized. And a simple consumption function for the individual is hypothesized:

(E:3) $$q = (a/p)^b,$$

where a, b are parametric constants, $b > 0$.

This consumption function states that, the higher the price of land, the less land the consumer will buy.

At any given location, then, equation (E:2) fixes the amount of money to be spent for land, and equation (E:3) determines the amount of land bought and its price when the equations are solved simultaneously. Thus functions $p(t)$ and $q(t)$ may be derived.

Thus far, we have presented the solution of individual equilibrium. Market equilibrium, in the case of a homogeneous population, is determined by

(E:4) $$n = 2\pi \int_0^{t_m} t/q(t)dt,$$

where n: total population.

This equation states that the population of the city is equal to the integral of the density of population $[1/q(t)]$ over the area of the city (assuming the simple availability of land function $S(t) = \pi t^2$). All elements of equation (E:4) are given, except for the limit t_m of the integral, and the equation is solved to find this distance, which is the margin of settlement. More accurately, equations (E:2, 3, 4) are solved simultaneously to find t_m, $p(t)$, $q(t)$, which constitute the solution to the problem.

The principal divergence between Mr. Wingo's theory and my own occurs at the outset. Mr. Wingo separates into independent compartments the preferences for accessibility (the dollar value of commuting time in $k(t)$) and for living space (the consumption function (E:2)). Prices and quantities are related within each of these two relations. In my approach, on the other hand, the preferences for land and accessibility (and other goods) are inter-related, and kept distinct from the budgetary considerations until they are joined in terms of marginal rates of substitution and marginal costs. All other differences between the two works seem to stem from this source. For instance, because in Mr. Wingo's approach the preferences for land and accessibility are not directly related, the assumption of the complementarity of rent and transport costs becomes necessary in order to reach a solution. Otherwise, there would be no way of determining land costs at any location.

Notes to Chapter 2

NOTE 1

From the budget balance equation (2:1), when $z = z_0$, we obtained

$$q = [y - p_z z_0 - k(t)]/P(t).$$

To observe how q varies with changes in t, we differentiate with respect to t, and obtain

$$dq/dt = (-P(t)dk/dt - (dP/dt)[y - k(t) - p_z z_0])/P(t)^2.$$

The quantity of land purchased increases with increasing distance as long as $dq/dt > 0$, and decreases when $dq/dt < 0$. Decreases in land will occur, therefore, when

$$0 > dq/dt = (-P(t)dk/dt - (dP/dt)[y - k(t) - p_z z_0])/P(t)^2.$$

Since $P(t)^2$ in the denominator must be positive, this condition will be true only when

$$0 > -P(t)dk/dt - (dP/dt)[y - k(t) - p_z z_0].$$

But, from equation (2:1), and $z = z_0$, rewriting,

$$P(t)q = y - p_z z_0 - k(t),$$

so that we may substitute and write

$$0 > -P(t)dk/dt - (dP/dt)[P(t)q].$$

Dividing through by $P(t)$ we have

$$0 > -dk/dt - (dP/dt)q,$$

which may be written as

$$dk/dt > -(dP/dt)q.$$

The interpretation of this is simple. Given a constant expenditure on the composite good ($z = z_0$), the amount of land decreases when the marginal commuting costs (dk/dt) exceed the marginal savings from the decreasing price of land ($[dP/dt]q$: where dP/dt is the decrease in price, and q is the quantity of land).

It is interesting to note that the units of the ratio of the derivatives of commuting costs and price should reduce to square feet. This can be seen if we rewrite the last inequation above as

$$-(dk/dt)/(dP/dt) < q.$$

(The inequation is reversed because $dP/dt < 0$.) The derivative of commuting costs, dk/dt, is in terms of dollars ($) per mile ($m$):

$$dk/dt : \text{dollars/miles} = \$/m.$$

The numerator of the derivative of the price of land, dP, is in terms of dollars ($) per square foot (sq. ft.), while the denominator, dt, is in miles, m. Therefore, the units are:

$$dP/dt : (\$/\text{sq. ft.})/m = \$/m(\text{sq. ft.})$$

Therefore, the units of $(dk/dt)/(dP/dt)$ are:

$$(dk/dt)/(dP/dt) : (\$/m)/[\,\$/m(\text{sq. ft.})] = \text{sq. ft.}$$

This is as it should be, since on the other side of the inequation is the quantity of land, q, which is also measured in terms of square feet.

NOTE 2

From the budget equation (2:1), when $q = q_0$, we have that

$$p_z z = y - P(t)q_0 - k(t).$$

We wish to find out under what conditions z will decrease with increases in t, or, under what conditions $dz/dt < 0$. Differentiating the above equation,

$$p_z \, dz/dt = -(dP/dt)q_0 - dk/dt,$$

When $dz/dt < 0$,

$$p_z \, dz/dt < 0 > -(dP/dt)q_0 - dk/dt.$$

Therefore, $dz/dt < 0$ when $dk/dt > -(dP/dt)q_0$. The expression dk/dt represents the marginal increases in commuting costs. The expression $(dP/dt)q_0$ represents the marginal costs of land *with increasing distance*. Since dP/dt is negative, when the expression is preceded by a minus sign it represents the marginal savings resulting from the decrease in the price of land with increasing distance.

G

Notes to Chapter 3

NOTE 1

Proof that the bid price function of the business firm is single-valued.

This may be proved by *reductio ad absurdum*. Suppose there are two bid prices for a given level of profits G_0. These bid prices are p_i and p_i', and $p_i' > p_i$. Examine now equation (3:10) in relation to equations (3:11, 12, 13). If the optimizing quantity of land for price p_i' is q_i', the term R could be reduced by $q_i'(p_i' - p_i)$ if the lower price, p_i, were bid. The term R would be the only term affected in the profit-determining equation (3:10), and the equality could not continue to hold. (G_0 is a constant; V is in terms of t and q, which have not changed; and C is in terms of V, t, and q, which have not changed.) Consequently, the function must be single-valued.

NOTE 2

Proof that two bid price functions corresponding to different levels of profit for the same firm will not cross.

Consider two bid price curves for the same firm: $p_f(t)\llbracket G_0$ and $p_f(t)\llbracket G_0'$, where $G_0' > G_0$. If they cross at $t = t_i$, so that at that location $p_f(t_i)\llbracket G_0 = p_f(t_i)\llbracket G_0'$, this would mean that at that location and at that price for land the firm can realize a profit G_0' or a profit G_0. G_0 should be, by definition, the maximum profit at that location at that price, so that the possibility of a higher level of profits G_0' would mean a contradiction in terms. Consequently, bid price curves for the firm do not cross.

NOTE 3

Derivation of the slope of the bid price curve of the urban firm.

The differentials of equations (3:10, 11, 12, 13) are:

$$dG_0 = 0 = dV - dC - dR$$

$$dV = V_t \, dt + V_q \, dq$$

$$dC = C_V \, dV + C_t \, dt + C_q \, dq = C_V(V_t \, dt + V_q \, dq) + C_t \, dt + C_q \, dq$$

$$dR = p(t)dq + q(dp/dt)dt.$$

Combining these differential equations we obtain:

$$0 = dt(V_t - C_V V_t - C_t - q \, dp/dt) + dq(V_q - C_V V_q - C_q - p).$$

Holding q constant for a very small change in t, so that $dq = 0$, we have

$$0 = dt(V_t - C_V V_t - C_t - q \, dp/dt),$$

from which,

$$0 = V_t - C_V V_t - C_t - q \, dp/dt.$$

This expression may be rewritten as

$$dp/dt = (V_t - C_V V_t - C_t)/q,$$

where dp/dt is the slope of the bid price curve.

H

Notes to Chapter 4

NOTE 1

Point $q=0$, $z=[y_i-k(t_m)]/p_z$ is under the curve in the z dimension (since $k(t_m)<y_i$). That is to say, it is within the domain $(0<D\rightarrow\infty)$ of the indifference curve. However, it is outside the range of the curve $(0<R\rightarrow\infty)$, since the q-co-ordinate of the point is 0. Given that the curve is convex toward the point and monotonic, only one tangent is possible.

NOTE 2

Residential bid price curves will be single-valued if at any location t_0 there is only one price $p_i(t_0)$ that enables the individual to maximize his satisfaction at precisely u_0. Given t_0, $p_i(t_0)$, and u_0, we can find the corresponding values z_0 and q_0. The following equations must hold:

$$u_0 = u(z_0, q_0, t_0)$$
$$y = p_z z_0 + p_i(t_0)q_0 + k(t_0).$$

Now assume there is a price $p_i'(t_0)$, smaller than $p_i(t_0)$, on the same curve. That is to say, there are two values of the bid price curve that enable the individual to reach satisfaction u_0 and no higher. Knowing t_0, $p_i'(t_0)$, and u_0, we can find the corresponding z_0' and q_0'. Since $p_i'(t_0)<p_i(t_0)$, the budget function

$$y = p_z z_0' + p_i'(t_0)q_0' + k(t_0)$$

must contain at least one point at which $z_0'>z_0$ and $q_0'>q_0$. Since both z and q are goods with positive marginal utility, and since t_0 is a constant,

$$u(z_0', q_0', t_0)>u(z_0, q_0, t_0) = u_0.$$

Therefore a lower second bid price for the same level of utility is impossible. By reversing the direction of the inequalities, it can be shown that a second higher price is equally impossible. Consequently, the curve must be single-valued.

Note also that the last inequality in the above argument shows that the lower price implies greater satisfaction.

Note 3

They cannot cross, for if they cross they must be apart elsewhere, and the lower of the two will give greater satisfaction. Should they cross there would be a contradiction, for the price at which they cross would enable the individual to maximize his satisfaction at a greater and a lesser level at the same time.

Notes to Chapter 5

NOTE 1

If the bid price curves are as shown in Figure 52, such that $p_f(t_2)$ $[\![t_3, P_3 < p_i(t_2)[\![t_3, P_3,$ but $p_f(t_1)[\![t_3, P_3 > p_i(t_1)[\![t_3, P_3,$ then i would

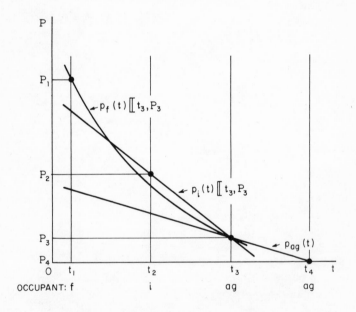

FIGURE 52. Special case of a nonadjacent marginal price-location

pay price $P_2 = p_i(t_2)[\![t_3, P_3$ at t_2, and f would pay price $P_1 = p_f(t_1)[\![t_3, P_3.$ All that has been changed from the case presented in the text is the referee of the firm's bid price curve.

Note 2

Relation of various rent concepts to the model: Economic rent is usually defined as the difference between the transaction price (what was actually paid) and opportunity costs. *Opportunity costs* are what the next highest bidder is willing to pay. Thus economic

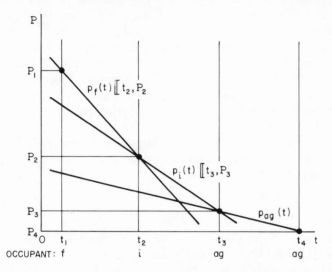

FIGURE 53. Equilibrium bid price curves and the price structure

rent is what the successful bidder must pay in excess of the next highest bid to secure the good (in this case, land at a particular location). In Figure 53, the economic rent paid by the firm, f, is $P_1 - p_i(t_1)[\![t_3, P_3$. Individual i pays no such rent since the price he pays is equal to the firm's bid at that location: $P_2 = p_f(t_2)[\![t_2, P_2$. On the other hand, if we aggregate the firm and the resident into an "urban sector," from the point of view of this sector the only competitor for land is agriculture, and the opportunity costs are $p_{ag}(t_1)$ and $p_{ag}(t_2)$ at t_1 and t_2, respectively. Therefore, economic rent of the urban sector is $P_1 - p_{ag}(t_1)$ at t_1 and $P_2 - p_{ag}(t_2)$ at t_2. Thus, while from the point of view of the individual there is no economic rent at t_2, there is one from the point of view of the urban sector. Finally, we may regard the firm, the individual, and the farmer as the "economy as a whole." From the point of view of the economy as a whole, there are no opportunity costs, and the economic rent is the full price at each location.

The meaning of location or situation differential rent will also depend on the point of view. The marginal price-location of f (that is, the referee of its bid price curve) is the price P_2 at t_2, and the marginal price-location of i is P_3 at t_3. Therefore, from the point of view of the firm and the individual, their respective location differential rents are $P_1 - P_2$ and $P_2 - P_3$. If we aggregate them into an urban sector, however, the margin of this sector will be location t_3 at price P_3, and, while the differential rent at t_2 remains the same, at t_1 it will be $P_1 - P_3$ for the urban sector as a whole. Finally, from the point of view of the economy as a whole, the margin is $P_4 = 0$ at t_4, and at every location the full price is location differential rent.

All of this is to say that when these classical concepts are used, great care must be taken to make clear the point of view one is referring to.

NOTE 3

We wish to prove that j's bid price curve through i's equilibrium price location, $p_j(t) [\![t_i, P_i$, will be less steep than i's equilibrium bid price curve, $p_i(t)$. We will abbreviate $p_j(t) [\![t_i, P_i$ to $p'_j(t)$. See Figure 28. By definition,

$$(I:1) \qquad p'_j(t_i) = P_i.$$

Considering equation (I:1) together with inequality (5:2), since an individual's bid price curves do not cross, it follows that $p'_j(t) \geqslant p_j(t)$ for any t. Consequently, at distance t_j, from equation (5:4)

$$(I:2) \qquad p'_j(t_j) \geqslant P_j.$$

Subtracting equation (I:1) from inequality (I:2)

$$(I:3) \qquad p'_j(t_j) - p'_j(t_i) \geqslant P_j - P_i.$$

The right side of inequality (I:3) is the same as that of inequality (5:5), so that we may write:

$$(I:4) \qquad p_i(t_j) - p_i(t_i) \leqslant p'_j(t_j) - p'_j(t_i).$$

From here the proof continues as it did after inequality (5:7) in the chapter. For the proof that $p_i(t)[\![t_j, P_j]\!]$—to be denoted by $p_i'(t)$—is steeper than j's equilibrium curve, consider that $p_i'(t) \geqslant p_i(t)$; by definition, $p_i'(t_j) = P_j$; since $p_i'(t_i) \geqslant P_i$, it follows that $p_i'(t_j) - p_i'(t_i) \leqslant P_j - P_i$. From here the proof continues as after inequality (I:3).

Note 4

Convex curves. If we met a curve more convex toward the origin than the normal curves and tried to solve for the equilibrium of the market by the method outlined for curves of constant ranking by steepness (chapter 5, section D), we might be misled into a false solution such as that represented in Figure 54. The convex curve, $p_c(t)$, would appear to be the least steep curve in the interval $t_3 - t_4$.

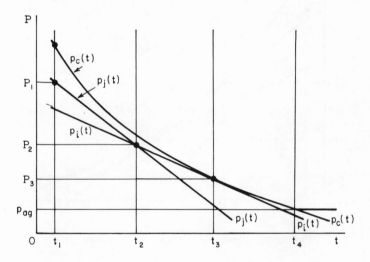

FIGURE 54. A possible error as a result of a convex curve

Thus, we might make the mistake of assigning individual c to t_3 at price P_3, based on the marginal price-location t_4, p_{ag}. Then, following the chain, individual i would be assigned to t_2 at P_2, based on the margin at t_3, P_3; and individual j would be assigned to t_1 at P_1, based on the margin t_2, P_2. But this would be an erroneous solution because the curve $p_c(t)$ is above the prices P_1 and P_2 at t_1 and t_2, respectively. Actually, two solutions are possible, depending on the degree of convexity of $p_c(t)$. The two solutions are shown in Figures 55 and 56.

In Figure 55 is shown the stable solution for the less convex situation. In this case c is at t_1, and paying price P_1. His margin is the next price-location, t_2, P_2. Individuals j and i are at t_2 and t_3, respectively, their respective marginal price-locations being t_3, P_3 and t_4, p_{ag}. In other words, once the correct spatial ranking c–j–i is discovered, the problem becomes identical to one in which the bid price curves retain a constant ranking in their steepness. We would

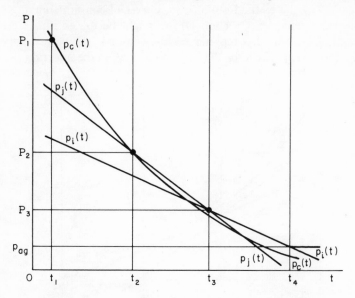

FIGURE 55. A possible solution with a convex curve

have arrived at this ranking by comparing the steepness of the curves if, instead of starting by finding the least steep curve at the margin of the system (t_4), we had found the steepest curve at the center (t_1). This would have been $p_c(t)$, and individual c would have been assigned to t_1. The rest of the problem conforms to the method of solution for curves of a constant ranking by steepness.

However, the problem of convex curves does not disappear by comparing steepness at the center. If curve $p_c(t)$ were more convex than is the case in Figure 55, we would arrive at an erroneous solution such as that shown in Figure 57, where the curve $p_c(t)$ is above P_3 and p_{ag} at t_3 and t_4 respectively. The correct solution for such a situation is shown in Figure 56, where the order c–j–i remains, but the marginal price-location which determines P_1 for c at t_1 is t_4, p_{ag}, not t_2, P_2. A less convex curve would have resulted on a margin at t_3, P_3, and one yet less convex, on a margin at t_2, P_2.

The situation may be summarized thus:

(a) The problem of spatial ranking of users of land diminishes for convex curves if we rank the steepness of the bid price curves at the center rather than at the margin.

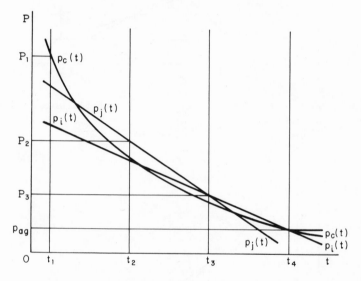

FIGURE 56. A possible solution with a convex curve

(b) The number of intermediate locations between the equilibrium and the marginal locations increases with the convexity of the curve for very convex curves; however, curves which are not very sharply convex will retain the adjacent rear location as their margin.

See also note 6, this appendix, for a method of handling sharply convex curves.

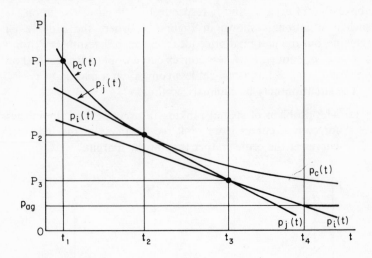

FIGURE 57. A possible error as a result of convex curves

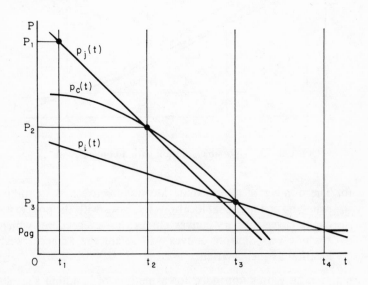

FIGURE 58. A solution with a concave curve

NOTE 5

Concave curves. Figure 58 shows an equilibrium solution containing one curve concave toward the center of the city. It will be seen that the concavity will insure that the curve will not rise above the convex price structure. The solution may be reached either by starting at the center and choosing the steepest of the unallocated curves at each location, or starting at the periphery and choosing the least steep of the unallocated curves at each location. Thus, we may start at t_1. There $p_j(t)$ is the steepest curve, and we assign j to location t_1. Of the remaining two curves, $p_c(t)$ is steeper than $p_i(t)$ at t_2, and we assign c to t_2; i is assigned to t_3. If we test the steepness of the bid price curves of the users not yet situated at each location (or, more accurately, for mean steepness between adjacent locations), concave bid price curves present no problem.

There is one exception, however. This is the case of concave curves that contain a very sharp break rather than gradual change. Such curves may result in a front marginal price-location as in Figure 59, or, as in Figure 60, they may retain a rear margin. In

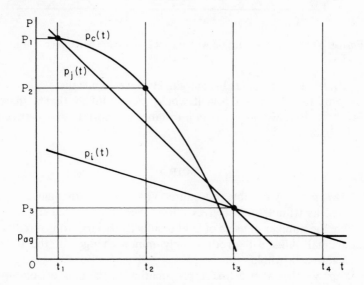

FIGURE 59. A possible solution with a concave curve: front marginal price-location

both cases, however, the equilibrium price-location of the user with the concave curve (t_2, P_2) is not the marginal price-location of the user in front of c. This individual, j, skips c's price-location and uses

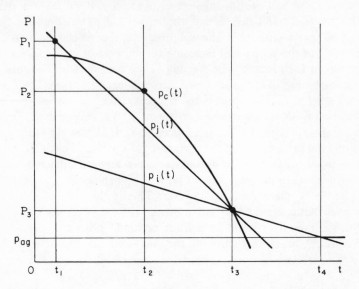

FIGURE 60. A possible solution with a concave curve: shared rear marginal price-location

t_3, P_3, to the rear of c, as his margin. However, while these cases are of some theoretical interest, it would seem unlikely that a sharp break in slope would occur in a distance as short as that between neighbors.

NOTE 6

Mixed curves. A sensible procedure to handle very irregular curves as well as troublesome convex curves can be suggested for cases where the number of users of land is sufficiently large to insure that individual shifts will produce only minor changes in the price structure as a whole.

Suppose that after a first approximation to the market solution there remains one curve which rises—at a few locations—above the price structure obtained, as curve $p_i(t)$ rises over $P(t)$ in Figure 61.

Find for this individual a lower bid price curve, $p'_i(t)$, equal to the price structure at one location (t_m) at least, and greater than the price structure at only one other location (t'_m). Then, in a second

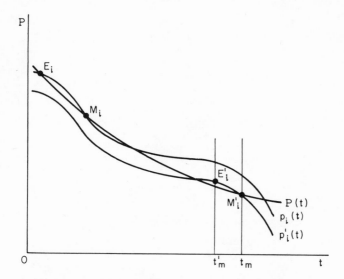

FIGURE 61. Method of solution with a mixed curve

attempt at the solution, the individual with the complex curve may be located by remembering that his marginal price-location will be the equilibrium price-location of the individual who occupied t_m in the first solution. E_i and M_i are the original, incorrect equilibrium and marginal price-locations; E'_i and M'_i are the corrected ones.

Index

Accessibility: and the minimum costs of friction hypothesis, 101–103; preferences, 26–27, 183–184; as source of rent, 5–6, 9–11, 15; given transport routes and many centers, 130–140
Assessed value, 170–171
Athens, 108n

Bartholomew, H., 2n, 110n
Beckman, M. J., 14–15, 108n
Bergel, E., 131n
Bid price curve: agricultural, 38; comparison of curves of residences, firms, and agriculture, 73–75; of the firm, 52–55; irregular shapes, 90–94, 195–201; notation, 52–54, 62–63, 74; residential, 59–71
Bloome, N. R., 3, 9n
Bopegamage, A., 109n
Boston, 10n, 11n
Budget: equation, 21, 180; line or surface, 175–178
Burgess, E., 9, 106n, 130, 131n
Bye, C. R., 3n

Caplow, T., 109n
Center of the city, 9–10, 18, 44, 134n; multi-centered cities, 134–140
Chamberlin, E., 8n, 42–44, 102
Chicago, 11n, 129n, 133n
Cities: American, 106–116; in developing countries, 109
City shape, 130–142
Composite good, definition of, 19–20
Consumption function, 14, 125–126, 168–172, 183–184
Creighton, R. L., 139n

Demand for land, aggregate, 36–37, 76–77
Density, *see* Income; Population growth; Site, size of; Zoning
Dorau, H. B., 9n, 13

Duncan, O. D. & B., 128n
Dunn, E. S., Jr., 4, 5n, 37, 38n, 98n, 135n

Ecologists, 9–11
Economic development, 105–116
Elasticity: income, 106–109, 126–127; price, 13–14, 110n, 113, 126–127
Ely, R. T., 6n, 8n, 13
Equilibrium: agricultural, 38–42; of the firm, 42–52, 56–58; market, 36–37, 76–100, 150–157; residential, 19–35, 71–73

Featureless plain, definition of, 17
Firey, W., 11, 18n
Fisher, R. M., 8n
Fogerty, F., 113n
Foote, N. N. *et al.*, 128n
Friction, costs of, 6–8, 11, 13, 101–105

Gist, N. P., 109n
Grebler, L., 128n
Guatemala City, 109n

Haig, R. N.: effects of transportation improvements, 113; highest and best use, 43n; relation to ecologists, 9n; relation of rent to location, 6–8, 13, 15, 183; his theory reexamined, 101–105
Hamburg, J. R., 139n
Harris, C. D., 130n, 137n
Hawley, A., 9–11, 18n, 106n, 115n
Hayes, C. B., 133n
Height of building, 4, 46n
Hinman, A. G., 9n
Hoover, E. M., 38n
Hoyt, H., 131n, 140–142
Hurd, R. M., 5–6, 7
Hyson, C. D. and W. P., 135n